Zsuzsanna Gahse, born in Budapest in 1946, has lived in Vienna, Kassel, Stuttgart and Lucerne, and is now based in Müllheim (Thurgau, Switzerland). Her literary work moves between prose and poetry, narrative and scenic texts. She has published more than thirty books, most recently *Bergisch teils farblos* (2021) and *Zeilenweise Frauenfeld* (2023), both with Edition Korrespondenzen in Vienna. A number of her stage projects have also been performed. To list only two prizes: she was awarded the Johann Heinrich Voss Prize of the German Academy in Darmstadt for her translations from Hungarian to German in 2010, and the Swiss Grand Prix for Literature in 2019.

Katy Derbyshire, originally from London, has lived in Berlin for over 20 years. Derbyshire translates contemporary German writers, including Inka Parei, Heike Geissler, Olga Grjasnowa, Annett Gröschner and Christa Wolf. Her translation of Clemens Meyer's *Bricks and Mortar* was the winner of the 2018 Straelener Übersetzerpreis (Straelen Prize for Translation), longlisted for the Man Booker International Prize 2017, and shortlisted for the 2019 Best Translated Book Awards. She occasionally teaches translation and co-hosts a monthly translation lab and the bi-monthly Dead Ladies Show. She helped to establish the Warwick Prize for Women in Translation, awarded annually since 2017.

Mountainish

Zsuzsanna Gahse

Translated from the German
by Katy Derbyshire

Mountainish

It ain't necessarily so

I

From the passenger seat on the drive from Venice to Munich, I saw the rock faces ready to collapse; above all, I saw their ability to collapse, and that collapse as hostility. Mile after mile of bare, rough, impersonal walls of stone.

These mountains never intended to contend as natural beauties, though people do like speaking beautifully about them. They say that they call, the mountains; the mountains are calling you. And yet all mountains have in mind is collapse, and that's no empty accusation; a person can be buried alive in the wink of an eye in the Alps, beneath scree, falling rocks, by avalanches and murky masses of mud.

The mountains are kneeling, even the three-thousanders and two-thousanders crouching and kneeling, and they pounce in the process. From inside a moving car, barely anyone will register the graunching and grinding in the rocky slopes, I assume, but a falling chunk of stone will suddenly hit the car roof, beneath which I'll be squashed flat after a short, sharp shock.

A drive through the Alps is not everyone's cup of tea.

The driver of the car was a fellowship-holder from Romania who, like me, had spent a short time in Venice, and since he spoke only broken German we were mostly silent, driving quietly through the brittle mountain ranges.

Nur Autos und Alpen, he said at one point, and we laughed, though I won't list the many different reasons why a person might laugh.

2

The Julier Pass, the one below the lumpen Piz Julier, is an ideal mountain crossing, the kind I'd wish for everywhere in the Alps and other highlands. Even on my first approach from the north, I liked this sedate pass. A comfortable road winds from west to east up to the wide col, and having reached the top I was relieved; on that very first approach I was surprised and relieved to find such a generous, open place. The road down to Engadin too, continuing eastwards, has its good moments. It is possible after all, I thought, to conquer mountains without fear and oppression. I shall set aside the geological aspect (granite, towers of chaotically stacked, unstable blocks), and since I was aware that even the Romans knew and loved this mountain crossing, I felt supported in the cultivated landscape named Julier after the Roman patrician family. Julius Caesar and the long-conquered area were mountainous reassurance.

Except that Julius Caesar or Romeo and Juliet have nothing to do with the Julier. Still, the harmless incline on the way up is as noble as the view from the top of the pass. There is a serenity up there, at least on clear days without snow or rain. And without the formidable view up to the Piz. Another good thing is when no cars approach, since drivers especially like the speed in the bends of the road, whether upwards or downwards. I am familiar with these muscle men and adrenaline junkies, not necessarily mountain-lovers, from the Furka Pass; I've made their acquaintance a number of times, including in fog. The vehicles would drive up inches away from my rear bumper, or from the person driving the car, who from their point of view obviously did not belong to the area or in the landscape, otherwise she would have driven just as fast as those behind her. They wanted to blow up the foreign driver (foreign body) in my car, those bend-drivers, bend-braggers, possibly with Alpine roots and thus likely racist, they wanted to point out to me that there are Alpine people and then there are foreigners, whatever their skin colour. Those were the kind of thoughts they had at the very back of their minds. Back then, perhaps not these days. And I too had my thoughts, as I drove on. But perhaps some of the pushy drivers were Dutch. Many people in Holland grow tired of their flat land and hurl themselves, ravenous, upon everything formidable, including the rocky Alps, where they like to prove they can cope with mountains' quirks and passes and therefore push away the more cautious drivers, scatter them. They almost latch on mid-switchback, nudging the car in front off the road, or they'll chuck a bomb into my car and overtake. The question is, who is the better speed freak; who is braver and more at home; above all, who is more at home? And a question like that is disturbing.

3

At the Furka Pass, I took a little walk and my dog walked ahead. He did not run away; he was just faster than me and then stopped by a path at the unpaved edge. I thought he was about to leap off the steep face, but he merely inspected the rock calmly, his expression alert.

4

Where is the wit in the mountains? Forget it.

5

Beautiful words like gneiss, flysch, quartzite, granite and

shale. Then there are things to point out such as copper deposits, salt sediments, possibly also gold deposits, and crystals and semi-precious stones are sure to be mentioned. These terms describe what is called the dead matter of the mountain regions, and some of the words awaken desire, which might even be called greed. Greed feels antiquated, but as long as the word is not overused I do like it, because it describes a craving that goes all the way to the gut.

Often, the various types of stone with their beautiful names lie close beside and below one another. They are a society of stones. They have to sustain (tolerate) one another, which does not always work and can lead to landslides and falling rocks.

Life leaps surprisingly into play in the dead rock, though it is emphasised as lifeless material, not just in limestone, in the Limestone Alps, in the deposits of living creatures, though those living creatures are not alive. Yet the deposits do at least contain former life.

One thing I especially like about moun-tains is all they con-tain.

But independently of the former life in limestone rock, frozen creatures lurk beneath the glaciers, thawing, breaking through, popping up as the ice masses retreat. Bacteria. Ancient, sleeping types of bacteria, unknown to date, awaken. It is seen in Siberia too, where the permafrost is also giving way.

Only recently have there been reports of unfamiliar bacteria, previously enclosed calmly beneath the ice mantle, quasi-lifeless. Now they are popping and plopping up, and this new word suits them. Perhaps they are harmless clowns that take pleasure from plopping.

6

At the top cable-car station, I started with a coffee while I watched the approaching and departing cable cars, and then I headed uphill, slipped and landed in a rocky hollow, a kind of dugout, and because both my feet demanded a pause after the slip, after the misstep, I sat down on the dirty, dusty ground, where no one had surely sat for a long time. I had no trouble with the view. I saw no steep rock faces nearby, the valley boasted pale-roofed, quiet houses, and I had a voluntary time-out of at least twenty minutes.

The only thing that was not beautiful or calming was the hairpin road contorting in tight bends, which I tried to overlook.

7

On a short residency in Venice years ago, I met a man who kept five different diaries in parallel. This fellow resident, a newly qualified architect full of zest for life, rage for life, must have had a quintuple brain.

In one of his diaries he listed each day's activities, in another he kept notes on conversations, and a third book was reserved for comments on architectural aesthetics, though these comments inevitably overlapped with the conversational notes. I cannot remember other content areas; all I know is that I found one of the books funny.

Perhaps he collected jokes as well, or his sexual escapades were amusing; this young man in Venice saw himself as something of a Casanova.

Those separate entries must be a drain on the brain, I thought at the time, and his thoughts seemed to me like single segments of an orange, but now I am interested in fragmentation like this, now I see it as a challenge. I could outdo him with a tenfold diary system, yet there is still something that troubles me about his books, probably the adamant way he explained them.

Aside from the architect, a philosopher was also staying at the house, a successful philosopher who had developed a system for centrally controlling traffic lights and was travelling the world with that system of his, all the way to India. To this day, traffic lights that change too quickly or slowly remind me of him; above all, I know that traffic lights have a philosophical background.

8

One of my thematically structured portfolios could contain portraits, and that is where I would sketch that philosopher named Gregor – his surname escapes me. He was no taller than me, very slim, inclining to skinny, dark eyes and dark bushy hair; he was always in motion, restless, I could say, and despite that restlessness he had carefree, relaxed lips. He and the diarist never appeared at the same time. The architect, usually wearing pale linen suits, was blond, tall and always spoke standing up; I cannot imagine him sitting down, though we – he, the philosopher and I – ate communally with three other residents because there was only one kitchen, where, incidentally, the unwashed crockery stacked up, and there would be plenty to say about that (some of us could keep separate notes on kitchen rotas, I suspect), and aside from that we had a communal bathroom with a single shower, which we used one after another and never communally.

9

From the train heading north from Milan, the surroundings looked subdued. Neat stone walls on either side of the tracks, now and then a gleaming giant in the distance, stoically eroding. An eroding giant. It sounds obscene. What was up with the mountain? Its head held high, something mountainish was happening to it in the distance.

In Brig we had twenty minutes to change trains; two of us were travelling together with the dog, not much luggage, so we could go down through the tunnel to the Rhône for a moment from the platform.

The Alps, the Rhône, the dog and a little green.

There was plenty more green in our immediate vicinity as we continued our journey, all sorts of deciduous trees, later conifers.

10

We were driving to Stels at the top of the Prättigau valley, the dog on the back seat, and once again I was evidently driving too slowly in the hairpin bends for the locals, though the road up to Stels is an easy drive compared to the Maloja Pass.

We could talk to seasoned drivers for days about the steepest, narrowest, longest bends in the entire Alpine region, trying to determine whether driving these stretches upwards or downwards is more impressive or unpleasant.

The road to Stels is not a comfortable one, and if the postbus comes along it is not clear at first which of the two vehicles will plummet, the postbus or your own car. The decisive factor is which vehicle is driving on the valley side. Cars on the mountain side can only be squashed. Everyone must have such conditions clear in their mind. I was driving upwards, a pale green sports car following behind me, inching ever closer, and eventually it latched on to push me uphill.

11

Who wants to see a full view of the Alps?

12

This respected mountainscape contains guesthouses, cabins, old and new hotels and pensions, and aside from a few blind, never-visited areas, it is a region where transient travellers can easily find a place to stop and eat.

13

Check under the bed, never trust the toothbrush glass. The floor is suspect, particularly if carpeted. If a personal message appears on the TV screen in better hotels, a welcome message especially for the guest, for you, with your name, then the message is pseudo-personal, the opposite of personal, purely technical, an intrusion into your business, dishonest from the outset. They want to control you, invade your privacy. Be careful what you do in such a room, including at night.

14
When I can't sleep I count up the hotel rooms I have stayed in so far. I take a topographical approach, country by country, city by city, town by town, including villages. So far, I have not stayed in an endless number of hotels.

15
When crossing the Alps, be it from west to east or in some other direction, travellers are mainly interested in the changing perspectives, which is the whole reason for tourism existing. One could claim that.

16
In Brig, the station forecourt is a starting point for seven postbus lines, including the route to the Simplon Pass.

The yellow buses arrive one after another from various departure points and depart simultaneously for their set destinations. It is a choreography easy to observe at many bus stations. I recently saw such a performance in the Jura, in Gelterkinden, where four buses in a row set out in single file like a gaggle of geese, huge birds migrating together through the small community, but all at once they parted ways and all four of them accelerated. That too was beautifully coordinated.

17
In Bergell, outside the Hotel Bregaglia in Promontogno, only two or three buses arrive simultaneously and the hotel

forecourt is not a bus station but a stopover; yet the postbuses depart together for their further destinations, and the hotel guest watching from a window might think the hotel's solidity had come about in parallel to the excellent travel service, which may be partly true, since the building was not designed with cheap guests in mind but for arrivals in chic hats and ankle boots, the kind everyone knows from film footage of days gone by.

18
Now I have invoked the well-known olden days of the Alps as advertising, seeing as the classier hotels present themselves that way, anyway.

19
The yellow buses' simultaneous arrival at various places and carefree departure is down to digital planning these days. The buses and thus also the drivers are carefully scheduled. Behind the choreography of arrivals and departures lies topographical knowledge of the area, bearing in mind different altitudes and obstacles for the drivers to overcome on each route, depending on the weather and depending on the roads and the tourist traffic. The calculation of the various bus journeys, which works perfectly down to the minute, can only be performed by philosophical mathematicians.

20
Which brings me once again to the successful young philosopher in Venice, a man I have lost sight of and would not recognise now.

For a while there was a shortage of philosophers, only two or three names of general philosophers were named, but the tide has since turned and there are now many specialised applied thinkers.

21

I am planning to live in a hotel room for some time. Postal address: Hotel Bergblick. Clean laundry is delivered to the room, breakfast awaits the guest in a bright space, with the added bonus of a friendly morning greeting from the waitress or waiter; otherwise, quiet prevails. Not a word falls upon the daily-tidied room or upon my papers on the desk by the window, with its eponymous mountain view.

22

This hotel, in which I hope to spend around two months, is located in a safe valley, no rocks collapsing above me.

A gigantic peak at an appropriate distance would not bother me. That is the difference from the horrific forms, called monsters for simplicity's sake, that display their catastrophic past through their vicinity, exerting a threatening effect. Their nearby unpredictability makes them monsters, and in contrast to them, even gigantic mountains in the distance are nothing but silhouettes of stone.

23

Vals. / I leaned on the high balcony / and light lay everywhere. / Up above, the peaks, / and I was down.

24

I spent three days in Lech. On the second evening the owner joined me at my table with a glass of wine, and we talked among other things of the difference between alabaster and plaster. At night I heard rumblings now and then outside and was troubled, not knowing the area or the noises.

On the second morning my hostess again brought me breakfast in bed. Breakfast in the room was something the pension offered. Here we have your breakfast, and I'm bringing you the sugar today in an alabaster bowl, she said, her tone confiding. Hot coffee, pale eggs from summer hens, pale bread rolls and summer honey.

Once I was alone again, I drew the curtains half-closed to spare myself the view of the craggy Hasenfluh, although since then I've faced more terrifying chunks of rock.

25

Below the wooded hills lie buildings with flower-cluttered balconies, and most of these balconies run all the way across the front of the houses. Someone waters the geraniums in the morning, and otherwise no one is to be seen.

26

Such houses with their elongated balconies are a component of a montane architectural fashion that has persisted for centuries.

27

After a terse climb to a peak, after a failed attempt, I have ended up in the village hospital. My room is lovingly decorated. A wooden bed, a painted wooden wardrobe. I have a balcony and on the balcony are geraniums, tended daily. Later, no one will be able to explain what I died of.

28

There are non-smoking rooms, non-drinking rooms, non-loving rooms and the stone peaks. Nothing but stones.

29

I shall try to find out, through a survey, who travels the Alps and why. I'll assume from the outset that many people would be ashamed not to travel, to stay at home, and they don't want to be ashamed when comparing themselves to others. They'd be embarrassed, they'd be down, and why should they labour with a predictable depression if they can instead toil their way around the Alps? Perhaps they are not aware that those in need can get support on the telephone, on the subject of travel taboos or geographical taboo zones. And even if they are already in the Alps and are feeling out of place and lacking orientation, upon their reluctant arrival, there is plenty of help to be had. In many cases, even individual mountain houses and hotels offer their support, finding the simplest routes back home for their guests.

30

The decisive factor is that the homeward-bound do not come into direct encounter with the enthusiastic mountain climbers and alpinists, and not because the rock-lovers would jeer at them, for instance. Such things rarely occur and are barely worth mentioning, besides which, any half-way healthy homeward-bound individual could simply jeer back. But despite their composure, the homeward-bound who have just abandoned the mountains would be bound to see boundaries between two types of natures, between those inclined towards mountains and those disinclined towards mountains. Suddenly, every party to such an encounter might think there were two basic types of people.

31

It's best to float up to the destination on balloons. The first step is to calculate how many gas-filled balloons are necessary for your own body weight, and then to select the correct clothing. Don pantaloons before affixing a baker-boy cap, followed by face paint. Wide, smiling mouth painted red, red button nose, and as the audience in the valley and on the slopes applauds, the clown floats up to the mountaintop.

Another means of transport in the mountains is the helicopter. Against blue skies and clear mountain silhouettes they resemble dragonflies, and when they appear above a mountain and fly downwards with their noses aslant, they too look parodic.

32

With Ruth and her friends Sam and Manu, I came from Brig to Leukerbad by helicopter. We wanted to see the Rhône valley from above; split between the four of us, the price was acceptable. We ought to treat ourselves to a thirty- or forty-kilometre propeller trip every five years, said Ruth. Plenty of places worth seeing are not far apart: Sitten, Interlaken or Thun, we just have to overcome the confusing mountain obstacles, and we'd have the best view from a copter. We'd even get to know the obstacles over time. Yes, and get addicted, said Manu.

33
We could not see the Rhône from the hotel in Leukerbad, just walls of concrete, man-made mountains, instead.

34
I drove up the Julier again to see the rock from close up and to sketch it. There were stones of different sizes by the side of the road, rocks that I could inspect with my magnifying glass. I had a folding chair with me, my dog sat alongside me and I sketched as best I could without looking up at the Piz.

35
I know that the highest peaks mean proximity to the sky. Up in the celestial vaults sit deities, and when we look up and yearn our way up, up, up to the peak, we are closer to the gods. What a beautiful old view of the world that is. We have abiding instincts for an old view of the world with no universe. Tales of mountains as pinnacles, with no universe around us.

The mountain regions are clearly visible on modern satellite photos. As such, partly as such, they are interesting, but seen from the perspective of Earth's history they are above all ruffles, pimples. Unsettled regions, catastrophes. People are constantly clambering up to the gods, and the closest they get to them is on Mount Everest. Up there is either nirvana or Eldorado or gold in the sky.

Or people clamber up to overcome the sky.

And all along, the mountains driven into the sky are

actually in dialogue with the goings-on in the Earth's interior; as such: in dialogue with the depths.

36

Mountain flanks with clear vertical or oblique lines. Often, these lines have a surprising kink, as though the entirety of the rock had been snapped, and sometimes the lines are horizontal (though this is trivial), the way the layers were originally deposited, without being subsequently shifted. I sketch them to get closer to them, and as I sketch, the stories – not harmless – through which the mountains came about become visible to some extent.

37

There are the self-overcomers and then there are the risk-averse. I can only shake my head at the audacious climbers prepared for the most outlandish of ascents; I shake it in shame because I do not understand those people, cannot understand that they have nothing better to do than climb; I scatter shed hair with my shock-headed shaking. Their strange successful distraction from current affairs is shocking, but shucks, some achieve decent TV audiences for their travails and their travels.

38

Should I be marooned on a mountain, I shall just sit there. Then I shall look around and see whether I'll go on living or not. I shall not attempt survival training in advance; I think it's an interesting idea but I do wonder whether such challenges are only accepted by people who have never balanced on the brink in a natural way. People rescued with great effort from swamps or fished out of the sea, or who have fled from wrongful imprisonment through underground tunnels aided (or unaided) by others, who have miraculously escaped torturers, climbed off operating tables half-sedated or looked down the barrel of a gun, seen the shooter's determined eyes before he fortunately missed his shot, run out of burning buildings and since had to live with horrific skin deformations, got locked in a morgue overnight and had hair white as snow when set free the next morning – these people are not great fans of survival training in the mountains.

39

Of course it's presumptuous to keep talking about crumbling mountains, about stony slopes I have never seen collapsing aside from in film footage and news programmes, meaning my negative images are nothing but supposition, but still I believe I have seen suspect slopes in the mountains, and I know that people (peoples, bands of transients, larger community groups) who migrated across the Alps thousands of years ago inspected the slopes very carefully in this respect, keeping a close eye on the boulders and scree, surely not fainthearted like me and all the more exact and experienced. In some regions they called the dangerous slopes gonda, with possible rockslides in mind; a gonda for them was a heap of scree, and they took pleasure in precisely naming types of ground. Yet settlements were later built on the sites Gonda and Gondo. Gonda has since been abandoned, while Gondo was buried under scree, not long ago, and Bondo, at least similar in name, was recently flooded by an avalanche of mud and rock.

40

Over the course of time I shall calm down, calm is a question of time anyway, and then I shall drive casually along the tightest of switchbacks and hairpins. To start with, I'll concentrate on the mountain folds in the atlas, then from a helicopter, and finally on the roads. I shall migrate across the Alps, my dog and I shall migrate across the Alps. We must expose ourselves to the mountains, cannot simply turn away. In any case, it's good that water issues from the Alps, and that there are valleys.

41

Manu rarely joins in with the mountain stuff. She's not much interested in hunks of rock, she says. What matters to her is her own location, her standpoint, the point from which she has the best view of goings-on. She sits in restaurants and cafés, roams the streets and crooked alleys and collects portrait photos. At the moment, though, colours are at least as important to her. More on that later.

42

More on that later is a quote with multiple sources. More on quotes later.

43

Portrait of Manu. She has high cheekbones, her eyes are narrow like two clearly visible strokes, and her face is heart-shaped. People sometimes say of Russian faces that they are heart-shaped because the face narrows at the chin, not pointed but slim. Manu's (non-Russian) face is darker than chestnuts, as are her fingers. Her fingers are usually simply together side by side. She does not spread them, does not speak a great deal with her hands, and she can bend those hands deeply from the wrist: she is double-jointed. When she takes photographs she hinges her hands up and down. She is rather tall for a forty-year-old woman, but younger women are often taller these days. She wears her hair very straight. She was born in Segovia, came to Lucerne as a young girl with her parents, and she is called Manu because her father, originally from Mexico, wanted the name. After training in Madrid, she spent two years in Hamburg and then returned to Lucerne, but she often mentions the bright light in Hamburg.

44

Perhaps she is not really called Manu; she has an amused look on her face every time she introduces herself. Then again, Sam calls her that too.

45

Portrait of Sam. He is darker than his older sister but has similarly narrow eyes, short slim bean pods. He is gangly, long legs and long arms. He likes moving his head by inclining it briefly to one side (I would have to show you how he does it). He never talks much, or let's say he never tells much, and he is rarely entirely serious. He dislikes too much seriousness.

Recently, he said without laughing that he was an architect, that was correct, but he had not built the Alps; if he had they'd look different.

His mother got her way for his name, he claims. He says he's a mummy's boy, Manu a daddy's girl.

46

In theory, encounters with overnight guests in hotels should be part of the portrait collection, but then again I have already started a folder (a journal) for the hotels, and now the two topics overlap.

47

Some hosts scrub their rooms-to-rent clean, not a stain nor a peeling spot on the wall escapes their gaze, the owners and their wives are lean and the rooms they rent out smell of freshly washed sheets. In the mornings the bread rolls smell delicious, proper rolls from the bakery, and for lunch they serve something home-cooked on the patio under the trees. And when a guest arrives in one of these country hotels he lies down in bed in his room, in the freshly washed linen, and doesn't dare move a muscle, lies stiff beneath the starched duvet cover for minutes and cools off, although it ought to be warm under the regulation eiderdown, but all of a sudden he thinks he is under surveillance by the cleanliness, feels infantilised by the immaculate purity achieved through so much elbow grease, and then he exclaims, calls out loudly that there is no pleasing him, that's just how he is. He could smash his head, walk into the wall. Why does nothing satisfy him, he wants to know. It's all over, he says, over, soon we'll be staring at him, soon he'll be straitjacketed because he's had enough of everything, even of cleanliness, and he's right about that, he says, this exaggerated cleanliness is unbearable, he's right, and that's the worst part of it all.

48

A man stands outside a budget hotel, enters with some hesitation. The building has not been redecorated for decades, the reception is tiny, like it is in pensions, a red lamp poised next to a bell on a small desk, an appealing older gentleman seated behind it. It costs a hundred and fifty Swiss francs a night; the would-be guest does not have that much on him. He has previously been into four other hotels, none of which he could afford either, and so he decides to spend the night on a bench; but he refuses to sink any lower than that. He intends to enjoy the exceptional circumstances and get himself a bottle of wine, because everyone sits on benches with bottles.

49

On Thursdays he went to the Rebstock, the city hotel. He did not go there every week, but when, then always on a Thursday. They would await him at reception with a key, he needed to say practically nothing, usually just nodding, and soon after that he'd disappear into his room. He would climb the stairs with a strange smile on his face, having taken the key with a smile, which was known at reception, and it was known as well that it was always on Thursdays that he came to the Rebstock. Herr Rüsch, they called him. It did not occur to anyone that Herr Rüsch has previously been a city-dweller, was a person who could not stand country life in the long run. On Thursdays he'd take a bus and a train from a village in the mountains to Lucerne, walk across the bridge over the lake, and once he arrived in one of the rooms (all differently decorated, all featuring pictures by contemporary painters and artists) he would work for a while or read, only leaving briefly. The next day, a Friday, he always had something to get done, and then he'd return to the mountains.

50
Postcard to myself: It rained and rained, hard. Car lights reflected off the road surface, in the right-hand lane red tail lights close together, in the opposite the glaring headlights.

51
Another postcard: Perhaps the notes I send myself are my basic diary. Absolutely blue sky. Manu and Sam photographed the hotel in Promontogno, in the publicly accessible rooms. Sam was interested in the hotel's architecture, early twentieth century.

52
Only a few footsteps away from the hotel, on the other side of the little River Bondasca, is where Bondo begins, where an avalanche of mud and rocks recently destroyed several houses. Our forebears had a precise evaluation of the situation. Here is the non-endangered Promontogno, and over there is Bondo.

53
Before Sam's departure for London, the three of us were on the Großglockner. Sam, the dog and I were on one of the less-frequented paths, ahead of us a man in an anorak, kitted out with good mountain boots, very well kitted, his rather light-looking rucksack dangling from his back. We had him ahead of us for a while, then he turned left off the path, slipped – we saw that much – and then after his misstep we saw him no more.

54
Deposits of several languages from earlier epochs can be

unearthed, but are not as obvious as the stone lines, the lines in the stone with their clear statements. Not many are interested in what the old slithers of language show, half-concealed; that interest has been knocked out of us. Nowadays it is better, almost cult, to pick up new phrases on shopping tours or paste together something new ourselves, soon swapping the words out for newer ones. At the same time, it is said that there are four thousand languages in the world today, or a hundred times that or even more, and then one could claim there are currently exactly as many languages as people. That would be a striking, impressive claim out of the blue.

Few can combat such claims. There is barely any money left for linguists, even for the major languages, and nothing for the small ones, nothing at all. At the moment the focus is more on national language variants, minuscule phenomena in individual countries. I shall come back to this.

55

I don't know the mountains, not really, I tell the hut warden. Before that I told him I'd been to the Furka Pass and the Julier and also to Leukerbad, but I don't really know the areas, I said, and he nodded and repeated Leukerbad. In Leukerbad, I know I don't want to take the cable car down to the Rhône and then up to the baths and then back down again. I was impressed there by the pebbly bed of the Rhône, that's true, the view of the Rhône is an abiding image, I said, and he asked me to repeat what I had just said; he had not understood me, and when he asked for the repetition I had to ask him what he had asked; he evidently did not understand me well and neither did I him, although after all this time in the country I like to think I understand all forms of Swiss German. Mere slivers, occasional syllables that perhaps make up an entire word fly past without me making sense of them, and that shreds the meaning of the sentence. My host had a similar problem with me, or worse, because he took no great joy in my language. He was friendly nonetheless, sitting with me on the bench outside the mountain lodge several times on the three days I spent with him, naming names of some of the closer, clearly visible mountains and repeating them, I assume mainly because he liked to have these local names in his head, the mountains above and to the east of Lake Uri, and I for my part repeated that I would sadly never really know the mountains. He did not respond.

He probably thought he had not understood me properly, but I was able to tell him, half-understood, about the older, worn, low mountains closer to my heart. He gave friendly nods.

I was the only guest in his mountain lodge. On the first day, he served me Älplermagronen, and since no one came by the next day we enjoyed the leftover pasta, the warden and I. Then I sat for hours in the simple room, where there was only a cupboard, a bed, two chairs and a decent table on which I could spread out my notes. I walked around the room barefoot on the clean wooden floor. Had there been rugs on the floor I would have moved them into a corner, but the bare floorboards had none.

In the mornings I went outside the lodge at five to see the peaks, which had not changed overnight. Only the light changed all the pointed formations, which I could barely memorise over those three days.

In the room, I spread out my writing sketches on the table, rearranging them several times. For me they are like photos are for other people, and as I arranged them I was reminded that some of the notes could latch on to one another and produce unexpected new meanings.

Since the warden had already asked me twice what I was getting up to for so long in my room, I almost told him about my folders and that I'd be starting a new folder alongside them for my yoked-together sketches. But because I did not tell him anything, he said he already knew. I was gfirchig, he said, afraid of the mountains, which I confirmed, and I admitted that I call the gigantic heaps whoppers.

To say goodbye, my host came out to the bench with two mugs of coffee, starting to talk even before he sat down. He spoke about the watersheds in the surrounding mountains, which are really worth talking about. I ought at least to look up the major watersheds in the atlas, I told myself. Aside from that, the warden told me about his Briäder, and it occurred to me that a woman I know in Lucerne once talked about her Brüeder, and I asked her how many brothers she had. One, she said, surprised. She did not understand my question, and now it turned out the singular of brother in Uri German, which I at least think I recognise, is Briäder. How the vowels shift! My host's further tales concerned him as a boy, and I assume that, after the details of his life, he wanted to know about my life only for politeness' sake, but since I'm not a life-story teller

I nodded as often as I could while he was speaking, and then said twice that I'd like to stay for a week sometime soon.

56

This time, I had to move on because the mountain house had been booked up for festival guests, months in advance. From June onwards, and even earlier, there are festivals from the far west to the easternmost Alps, have been for years now. These events are not restricted to the Alps but they do crop up in the mountains like mosquito bites, and so as not to give the impression that these bites are insignificant, a large audience is drummed up by inviting many guests for appearances, some famous, some less famous; it's the numbers that count.

57

Briäder, then. The vowels fly through the mountain skies, scraping against the higher rocks so that an *ü* changes into an *i*, a *u* to an *ü*, an *au* to a long *a*, an *i* into a clear *i+e* or *i+ä*, so instead of lieb the word is then li-äb, and the consonants incline away from the vowels or plummet and fall.

58

Neither the vowels nor the consonants fly only in the mountains; they also buzz across lower landscapes to the north, and some call the words' stopovers – where they display a sound variant – autonomous languages. Tricks like this make it easy to speak of ten thousand languages in total.

59

My days of rest in the mountain lodge made me more blasé, so I thought less often of the climbers on the cliffs. At Lake

Uri (High German: Urner See, Swiss German: Urnersee) they venture joyfully, cheerfully up the vertical stone walls, climbing in lonely silence even when not being filmed, but increasingly they are being filmed. Either way, they clamber up the steeply soaring rocks. How do they finance their tours? Are they mountain-climbing mendicants? Candidates yearning for a self-imposed death penalty? Is the mountain an opponent they want to overcome?

60

When I first met Sam, he showed me his tape recordings from various parts of the Alps, and he has a good place for these audio documents: his sister's studio in Altdorf.

In his recordings, the German in the Alps seems to contort more than the French or Italian. We shall see whether that impression can be upheld. In the meantime, we wonder how which languages contort and why.

61

Do languages depend on their environment? Are there languages in mountainscapes or valleys that are immune to their surroundings? Do people there say what they like, in fog and in rain and in the bitterest of dryness, and are always understood?

No one says bitter dryness, Ruth said. You say bitter cold.

Bitter cold makes your mouth freeze up, you might think, but that's not the case. People go on speaking in all cold zones. Where there are people, they speak; perhaps a touch less in great heat and cold.

62
In some languages, said Manu, everyone's throat has to switch over to start singing, and in other languages singing is always present, lurking in wait.

63
At lunchtime, six of us went to Restaurant Bergblick. We read the handwritten menu on a blackboard outside. Flan, for example. Flan: the perfect dish for everyman. The waiter brought me and Ruth a good schnitzel and then suggested taking photos of us, of his own accord. He wanted the freshly served plate in the picture. He was obviously long accustomed to the area and thus a local, but he was not a native. I like saying native. When I asked him where he came from, he told me to guess. I know this game. I often ask waiters where they're from and then I have a trump card up my sleeve because I'm from elsewhere as well, which I can mention so as to exalt them as Europeans, they and I are Europeans, and if Europe is not enough then I try to explain my connection to Asia.

I guessed that he came from the east. He had that eastern self-confidence, a comfort in his own skin and a friendliness that he gave us; he gave it to us as a gift, but at the end of a day's work, God knows what he thought about friendliness.

No, he wasn't from the east, he was from the south, he said cheerfully, now seeming like the owner. I responded with Italy and Spain, though the man did not appear Italian or Spanish to my eyes. (He appeared in my eyes, so I do have to mention my eyes.) No, no, our host said. Much further south. Everyone at our table took a guess. Algeria, Egypt. Much further south, he said with a laugh. His parents came from Turkey. For him, Turkey was deep in the south and not in the east. That poor man in the Alps.

64
Six-way conversations in the Alps; six is better than twelve, but the main thing is you see one another, see the faces, the eyes, each person's gait. The only real conversations, though, are between two or three people.

65
In six-way conversations, one person has to be a secret facilitator to drive the conversation forward. Or six people could give one another a thorough delousing.

66
As a snowstorm brews, six of them sit tight in a mountain cabin. Bit by bit, much of the roof is blown away, and what happens then?

They will not be rescued; they now will rest (so let it be with Caesar). Their survival training in the mountains has come to a bad end. And yet they did not call their ascent survival training. What did they call it?

Later, the warden at the lower mountain house, where they'd spent the previous night, spoke of a small group, of a gang.

These groups have always existed, independent of the mountains. Some set out together. And these six people will now be carried to their graves.

67

In lifts, the load capacity is usually stated in kilograms, along with the permissible number of persons. The most frequent number is six. I stand in a lift and think, 'Six Persons in Search of an Author', thinking of Pirandello's play.

68

Three persons start off for the Graustock, one falls, and then there are two.

69

Is a six-way conversation possible? Sam asked again, and Manu said that every person was sure to have a distinctive voice in conversation. So problems would only arise if the six of them were part of a single family, since then they'd share the same pitch of voice, and even speech tempo is adopted approximately from one generation to the next.

We've discussed this before, I said, we've talked about this once before. But never in detail, said Manu, and we could talk about it endlessly. The voice story starts strictly in the family and goes on in the regions. Aside from that, she said, she often saw someone on a bus or a train approaching another person and asking outright where they came from. Wo kommscht her, they asked. And then it turned out that the respondent had their language instilled in them five kilometres away from the enquirer. People have ears for the smallest of differences. That's why it was alright for me to ask waiters and waitresses where they're from, she said, otherwise it wouldn't be alright. Ruth just laughed.

They ask me because of my skin, not because of my language,

so there's no need to talk much about that, added Manu.

70
People have ears for the finest of differences and are addicted to language. In many cases, they don't even notice how addicted they are.

71
The sounds flutter in their ears; everyone listens closely. They sit on the train and pick up new words: first that, and secondly, they hear precisely who's not one of them.

72
Portrait of Ruth. As well as Sam and Manu, it was through Ruth that I met the weather narrator, whom I shall tackle in a separate booklet. We could trace all common acquaintances back to Ruth, as we do with the propagation of epidemics. She is a key person, a spreader.

73
The hotel, where I spent only one night, had its heyday some time ago, but the lakeside location with its view of a soft mountain silhouette is beautiful; behind the house is a gentle incline. On all three floors there are two or three seats and a little table in the hall, ready and waiting for one last drink before the guests retire to their rooms. Almost everyone arrives by boat, and that has always been the case; no one was carried here in sedan chairs, as was unavoidable in the higher mountain hotels.

How did the arrivals feel to be carried in sedan chairs in the rough, rocky zones! An incredible image! People clad in tweed and mohair with soft leather shoes, carried by the local inhabitants, and the latter are glad of the work, pleased to welcome visitors; they spare no effort, and the people in the sedan chairs lean back and look around.

Then the guests disembark from their chairs, are accompanied to their rooms, and there or in the large salon they write their diaries, some of which are now secured in archives.

74
Those diarists, conquerors with friendly smiles also known as colonists, sent postcards from the hotel too, tourist post. Words change, and we change with them. That is an almost correct quote from the Latin; correct would be: Times are changed; we, too, are changed within them. I am not sure whether the adage is true in every regard; I suspect not. Words change; we don't really.

75
Incidentally, the emergence of tourism is not far removed from industrialisation and Marx. This is a note for which I will not start a separate folder.

76
In the lakeside hotel, we sat on nice old chairs on the second floor, surrounded by green pot plants; Manu went on talking about language differences, Ruth nodded, and this time my dog lay beside her, sprawled upon her right shoe.

77
At around eleven in the evening, three thoroughly made-up women and two gentlemen of differing ages went into one

of the hotel rooms. All three women had pretty handbags. At around twelve, the little group went down the stairs; one of the women opened the door to another room, into which the five of them vanished.

78

I had to move out the next day; the hotel had been booked up long before, for a festival.

79

With a fifty-franc stake, I had hit the jackpot at the beginning of last year and was one of the few lucky winners who got to spend a year migrating through Alpine hotels free of charge.

80

That is wishful thinking, but there are not insignificant hotels that extend comparable invitations. They bring in singers, writers, philosophers, not necessarily the most famous but instead the ones that interest them or their middlemen, and often the invited guests are makers of niche literature or niche music, perhaps hiding places for what is secretly being sought.

81

Three years ago, I was in a hotel of that type in Engadin. The audience consisted of ten guests and the hotel's owner. The poor host with his well-meaning attempt, the poor presenter who had picked me from the pot of not-exactly-famous writers.

82
A storm raged. Flooded roads, falling rocks, landslides, flowing mud, the news reported. We were warned to steer clear of rivers and watch out for falling rocks and debris on the roads. Disasters in the heavy mountain groups, mountain ridges.

83
Sam regretted being unable to rebuild the Alps. He wished he could repair individual peaks, stabilise a good few rock-faces. The Alps aren't volcanic, he said, so you can't look down into their maws, they have no gullets. But their gigantic bodies are layered full of caverns, grottoes, shafts, mines, and then there are the tunnels. Sometimes he thought one of the mountains might collapse in on itself, he said, and that happens anyway in the fine detail, not just in the salt-works when the salt miners look for new salt stocks inside a stony belly.

84
Astute experts drill their way into the mountains, they hew the flanks into terraces, know all about rocks and their veining. Deep down in the mining tunnels of the Limestone Alps slumbers ancient sea salt. A grey shade of pink.

85
Exposed to the weather, the sheep of the Salzburg region graze in the mountains. They eat herbs at high altitudes, which makes their meat tasty, so that after their slaughter, generously portioned pieces need only roasting, barely seasoning. In the oven, basted with a little water since wine or beer would falsify the flavour, the roast takes three slow

hours and then you get a lamb-flavoured poem on your plate.

86

Aside from that, the mountain skirts are hewn away in terraces for cobblestones. First the rock-getters sledge separate blocks out of the skirts, split them into transportable chunks and then deliver them in wagons to the masons, who chisel the chunks into wieldy cobbles. As they hew, they must spot the stone's seams, its inner qualities, its fine veining, and that can be done only with instinct, experience, with good eyes and great strength. The masons hit out, and, as if it had waited for their precise blow, the stone falls cleanly in two. The finished cobblestones are pushed on rails to the funicular tram for further transport and taken down to the valley in cable cars. I've seen this quarrying of flysch sandstone in a film, and I quote that both the rock-getters and the masons often had black lung.

87

All this lifting and lowering, all these ropes and cables. It started with rope-lifts for mountain mine workers in grey dusty tubs. There are black-and-white films of those early days. Cable cars and chairlifts have been added since then, for two or more people, brightly coloured, easy-clean and a fine transport service for arrivals; there is no need for sedan chairs these days – but this cable-car world was not originally invented for the waving mountain tourists now smiling at the camera. Their smile is their gift to their hosts.

88

Years ago, I stood in a car park at the northern end of Lake Uri (Swiss German: Urnersee; High German: Urner See), and as I looked around I saw some kind of crate floating rather high in mid-air, moving gradually away from the mountain face. The crate was hanging from a revolving rope, and on the downward stretch the crate was heading for the car park, with the opposite strand on its way up the mountain. The rope-lift stopped not far from my car, and out of the crate climbed an unconcerned elderly person, perhaps around eighty. A few metres along, she got into a red vehicle and drove off.

89
It was a long time ago; that old woman must be dead by now.

90
Had she spent her childhood on the mountain, that trip on the rope would have been quite natural to her, she needed only bear in mind the wind and the weather. Perhaps, though, she came from the lowlands or the plateau and had fallen in love with a mountain person and plumped from then on for the crate-lift. Love in the silent Alps or silent love in the Alps. All at once she had mountain fever, which is infectious, I often hear. Stories like this, related by necessity to resettlements and readjustments, are best discussed with Manu and Sam.

91
Moving from the mountains to the plain would be a challenge too, and it would be unfair not to respect such a problem; my own well-being, though, is tied to vast landscapes, and I would like to assert my opinion that the ideal landscape is vast. The vast domain. Perhaps with a lake or a river nearby, an eroded low hill within eyeshot.

I used to think I could only ever live in a city, in one of the cities I knew; I would retire to a café every afternoon and indulge in conversation, would regard these deliberate and coincidental chats as relaxing or stimulating, and simply roaming the streets would be fine by me too. That's over now, and that *over* is part of the readjustments.

92
You get reknitted, Sam says about it, sewn up all wrong. Turned inside out, outside in. Sometimes he and Manu have Spanish landscapes at the back of their minds, Castilian, they say, and they compare the regions here with them.

93
Someone gets resettled, and now he's there, there he is, says Manu. From Lake Lucerne to Greenland, from Angola to Kyiv, where he learns the meaning of fear, from New York to Bergisch Gladbach. Or someone moves from Cairo to the Alps, then to London and back to the Alps. Relocations like that would work well in a flip book.

94
And amid the mountains stand rock-acquirers, rock-obtainers, rock-getters.

95
On one side of the Julier Pass is a granite region; on the other side the Julier Alps, harsh limestone formations. The Julier Pass is not related to Julius Caesar but the Julier Alps certainly are, though the harsh, inaccessible Julier Alps were not nameless even before Caesar captured them,

and everything that has a name can be proud of having been named.

96
After walking the dog, I sat outside La Corona restaurant by Lake Walen and noted down mountain names of the colourful kind. *Wei*sshorn, *Rot*henfluh, Ober*rot*horn, Uri *Rot*stock, Großes *Grün*horn (4,043.5 metres high), Monte *Rosa*, Mont *Blanc*. A Grünhorn must be green, and a Rotstock red.

97
Most people pay attention to their surroundings and observe them in all light conditions. When a particular mountain is constantly swathed in Nebel – that's fog – they'll speak realistically of a Nebelhorn, and a Rotstock won't be called red for no reason.

98
They will say: Rotstock, I gave you my heart, I gave you your name, and it is meant as a dialogue; and at the same time they also give others an indication of their own position.

99
Copper red, bright white, above them blue, azure blue. Indigo is darker. Azure means sky and sea and a documented human right to yearning. Indigo is more private, more suspect. Dark green (Scottish green, without intending to break out of the Alps with the word Scottish) appears in the deep calm brooks.

100
The calques in the colours. Azure originally meant not sky but stone. Indigo too is a loan word, as is beige. Soapstone, which can be scratched with mere fingernails – if a person has strong fingernails – is yellowy beige and was quarried centuries ago on the border between today's Switzerland and Italy.

101
As a result of excessive quarrying in Plurs (now Piuro), Monte Conto (a strange name that reminds me of Gondo) was so destabilised that an avalanche occurred in 1618. More than a thousand inhabitants lost their lives, the town was destroyed, and the documents of the time indicate that Plurs became famous worldwide (which will have meant Europe-wide).

102
It is interesting that the avalanche in Plurs was generally known, if only because the Thirty Years' War had begun three months previously with the famous Defenestration of Prague. It would not be surprising if apathy had hence prevailed towards natural disasters in the south of the Alps, but the snow-sliding occurrence was generally known.

103
On the plummeting Monte Conto, might I add that the name of the mountain might prompt thoughts of all kinds of counts and accounts. Before the avalanche, soapstone had made Priul a rich town; nonetheless, the word Conto is not related to banking. Both the Italian conto and the German word Konto mean bank account and come from

the Latin computare. To add up, to calculate. To amputate, by contrast, is to take away. And Monte Conto had its name before rock-getters started quarrying soapstone.

104
At this point, I would like to dedicate an ode to etymologists. Without their pointers I would often lack orientation, not only in the Alps.

105
Colour is not just a good cue for the mountains: salmon pink, lime green, rust red, egg-yolk yellow, lemon yellow, olive green or granite grey play a role in other regions. These colours can certainly be seen in the mountain forests and pastures, even though all I have in my mind's eye is the stone on the mountain flanks.

106
Other colours come into play inside the stone. Emerald, topaz, agate.

107
Spare a thought for rosacea-afflicted rock climbers: one moment they feel down about their pink skin, and then they misstep and fall out of the picture.

108
Red(dish) ochre is a prominent feature of cave paintings. Not only are the powerful bulls and proud horses ochre-coloured and blood-red, but also their hunters, beautiful masculine black or yellow hunters.

109
Only once in my life have I seen an albino person, a person with really white skin. As a child, I was in the changing room at a swimming bath and a young woman next to me removed her bikini to dry herself off. Even her nipples were white.

110
The unknown colours of all imaginable human nipples. What are little girls made of? Soapstone, spice, all things nice.

111
I recently heard about a yellow world.

Sour-lemon world and honey-yellow sunrise through fog, acrid yellow all around the world.

112
Four people in the fog, on a wide road, all of them little more than shadows. They are standing fairly far apart, three of them barely moving; the fourth, at the front right of the picture, strides slowly towards the viewer and transforms into a dark-red rectangle, or in fact is immersed in dark red, while the other three are contained in an unsettlingly foggy yellow-red. At the back this yellow-red, at the front dark red.

113
Inside a large brownish-green square is a story, now pried open with a crowbar.

114
Below twelve coloured spaces is a square, which could be said to have no colour, if there were such a thing as non-colour.

115
There's no point mistaking light brown for umber or black, Manu says, not laughing. She's dark chestnut brown, she says, her skin tone is chestnut brown, Sam is a tad darker but not black, and my skin, she tells me, has a touch of steamed salmon.

116
In my mind I had sounds like hackneyed mountain-and-valley music plus the latest hit tunes, and the dinging of the cable car, the noisy disembarkers, the noisy embarkers, screeches in the peak restaurant at the top cable-car station, children granted freedom to screech, and the other people's laughter was an imperative.

117
As always, Manu photographs individual faces or smaller groups. Later she will enlarge the photos in her lab in Altdorf.

118
We were outside Manu's studio on the ground floor, where Sam played me various recordings he had gathered in the mountains. People even have their own words in different regions, he said. Everyone can imitate several ways of speaking but it's better to stay in your own place, not resettle, because then every word is clearly marked, he said.

119

The church bells chime out long and loud at noon in the Christian Alps – as in all Alpine lands – dotted with their spires in aerial photos. There is no valley, barely a slope without a church tower; the only thing we cannot see in the pictures is the chimes. Tall crosses are also often installed on mountaintops. The entire mountain region is riddled with churches and chapels, with crosses on mountaintops, and then there are the crosses for those who plunged to their deaths.

There is no booming of falling rocks in photos, and everyone must imagine the roar of the waterfalls for themselves. In documentaries, classical Christian-sounding music tinkles through the rocks or inside the mountains. The stubborn peaks have been converted.

On this spring morn come blow your horn, but where are those boys who look after the sheep?

120

The Alps have team spirit, a feeling of togetherness, or at least they do in the various massifs.

121

I call the hulking giants whoppers, Manu calls them hunks; Ruth laughs. She stops in a mountain chapel and lights a candle. She places great faith in her candles.

122

Theoretically, a person could memorise the shape of every single mountain and still mistake the shapes for one another.

123
To begin with, I sketched the contours of the high and low Dachstein from pictures on the internet, then the Jungfrau massif, and after that I was in the Auvergne-Rhône-Alpes region in search of the French Alps. I have trouble with the complicated shapes of the Zugspitze; Sam will help me with a simplified model.

124
On northbound flights from the southwest, all I perceive is a jumble of white peaks. I get a step further en route from Vienna to Zürich. It is easy to spot Innsbruck with its valleys from the plane.

125
Every single pass is a hit, a bingo in the brawny mountain ranges, a crossing aid.

126
The Dachstein, the Aletsch Arena, the Rhône Alps and Mont Ventoux share a team spirit.

127
Sam was drawing, and he spoke as he did so of the structures of individual mountain masses, of splintery and stable blocks, of notches, recesses, nicks and drill holes in the massifs. On a second sheet of paper, he sketched a weighty mountain in cross-section, showing individual cavities. Rail tunnel, military accommodation, air-raid shelter, water culvert and so on.

128
Near the valley station on the mountain railway, there was talk of high fog and an approaching drop in temperature, combined with storms once again because the west wind was blowing. I had this information from Lucius, the weather narrator. Weather events in the southern Alps were insignificant, he said, there was nothing exciting due there; the south would be spared.

129
At the valley station, the cable cars arrived with a clatter. As soon as they were empty they were automatically steered into a waiting position so as to return uphill. Manu photographed the people in the queue, who looked like they were queuing for a carousel. They wore broad smiles and all of those waiting together laughed audibly. Tour buses arrived and departed directly outside the valley station, so the arrivals approached in groups and left again in groups. At the same time, several hundred people strode past the car park, waving flags. Azure prevailed in the sky. Two paragliders descended from above. The works, as the police like to say in crime shows.

130
The more extensive Manu's photo collection of laughing and grinning mouths gets, the more intensely she asks herself why people pull faces. We have talked about it before. Yes, smiles and laughter do more than signify joy. The triggers are more complicated. They can be about ridicule, cruelty or simply a kind of courtship or soliciting of interest, and all soliciting involves a pretence of smiling. Aside from that, laughter can bring others to a halt.

These days, Manu restricts her photos to the eyes, then mouths, then she will superimpose a strange pair of eyes above a mouth to see the resulting coherence or incoherence. When she photographs individuals, however, each shot must speak for itself. She doesn't comment, has no wish to interpret anything into the images. A picture is a picture and speaks for itself, she says.

131
A certain lack of focus often shows more of a person than precise illumination, she says, and portraits are sketches.

132
Anyone and everyone can be raised to smile constantly, depending on the country, and perhaps one can categorise laughing behaviours according to country; but a simple categorisation is not possible, only mixed categorisations: another reason why we will never come to the end of our conversation.

133
On this subject, I will add that Ruth only smiles with her eyes, almost never showing her teeth; however, in her circle of friends, where she is the core individual and the connecting link, various types of laughing and smiling occur. She has different friends and acquaintances and tries to connect them all.

134
One of the few mountain climbers I have met personally is Lucius, the red-blond young man with the tousled head of hair. He climbs up towers and steely technical installations

too, and even climbs down into caves. He's a mountain man born and bred, says Ruth, and she admires his weather skills. That's why she calls him the weather narrator. He is supple, has a flat stomach, and all interest from women and men bounces off him unnoticed.

135
His uncle, redder-headed than him and many years older, can be found in Altdorf every afternoon, at the Tell monument or in the courtyard of the Kunsthaus. Every day, as he paces back and forth, a few schoolchildren visit him. They ask him to solve complicated maths problems. Recently, a boy wanted to know what was three thousand and seventy-three times two thousand four hundred and fourteen. The red-headed uncle nodded and paced slightly faster than before, flicking his thumbnail against his middle finger as always. He soon had the solution. The boy laughed and told him he'd just multiplied the height of two mountains, multiplied two mountains: the Bristen and the Bälmeten.

136
In a mountain house, in an attic room, a man calls for help. Next door, another man calls for help. In the next room, an old woman stands by the window and calls for help. And a call for help is heard from the next-but-one room as well. In the room next to that, someone throws a radio out of the window and then everyone screams.

137
All of a sudden he is unsettled, starts pacing, gets faster and faster, and faster again, and another man walks very fast by his side, both pace to and fro, stretch their arms

up in the air, about to burst, probably egging each other on or their mutual unsettledness grows, and those standing around them want to know the two men's current blood pressure, when one of them and, soon after, the other slows down. Yet they do not slow their pace equally. In between, one of them and then the other has a brief burst of acceleration before they both come to a final standstill.

138
Suddenly, everything is beginning to become significant.

139
The festivals hunch on the mountains like red mosquito bites. No one has to seek them out, the invitations come flying on flyers, no matter whether the attractions on offer are artists, musicians, writers or theatre people. Often the flyers and posters boast twenty or thirty names, a whole bevy of artists, plus the names of the organisers and the sponsors' logos.

No one would drive a single cow up to the high pastures.

High visitor numbers have a magnetic power of attraction, even affecting future plans.

140
Guest performances in the mountains. Could go well, could be fatal.

141
At the end of the village of Poschiavo, several people were sitting in the middle of the road, others were standing

around, and I was walking up and down with my dog. We were all looking in the same direction, towards the south, that is, where a man in a city suit turned up in the late afternoon, having been walking all day in this outfit (a suit is a Gewand in Swiss German, which for High German- speakers is a robe). He had set out in Italy, marched for hours across difficult territory while holding up an impressive flag. In large letters, it said Il Contrabbandiere. On arrival at the waiting crowd his performance was over, a performance saluting the former smugglers and their arduous treks across the Alps.

On the road where the audience had waited, polenta was cooked in the evening and eaten with red wine. No one from the media was there, as far as I remember. The performance was the reverse of a mass event.

142
All hotels and guesthouses were fully booked for the next few weeks, I was told once again.

143
I backed out of the trip to the Schafkopf outside Salzburg; I cancelled the booking because I had a stomach bug, but also because I was suspicious of the complicated journey.

144
Besides, I cannot collect all the mountains. People do not like to move from the northern side of a massif to its southern side (or vice versa), while I for my part cannot be constantly travelling to visit them all in their places, to gauge every area.

145
Once, an acquaintance from the Baltic spent a day driving us around. He showed us the landscape that was all his, and that haughtiness took a different form in the north to that in the mountains. Haughtiness in different landscapes is an interesting subject.

146
Does it feel good to start living in a place? Or does living only feel good later, once new habits form? Or is it good when habits no longer feel new? Does all living feel good? Always troublesome? Enough to drive you up the wall? Would it be best to keep moving on endlessly? In a camper van?

Do you love a house most when you have to move out?

Would you like to have a loft in the middle of New York, looking down on Central Park in the morning and later strolling over to MoMA? Or is it dangerous to live in the centre of a city? Better go straight back to the mountains!

147
Instead of memories of Salzburg's surroundings, I have my memory of planning the trip. The backfired planning is also a story to tell.

148
Assuming a person throws away notes. They were there before and now they are gone, but since they were there once, they are not lost entirely. The seven hundred or more

notes are in the trash, or have been burnt. No one would have had time to read them all, anyway, not even us. We burnt them, the ash flew through the air, settled on things, and scientists have made this pulverised legacy visible again through minutely detailed work.

149
Since the notes were once there, they are still here (since there, hence here). Notes not possible to translate are unusable, and from my point of view anything untranslatable is as terrifying as the impassable regions in the Alps.

150
The following outline would be possible: First, a person thinks of greening nature and breathes a sigh. Second, they breathe a sigh at the sight of greening nature, thinking of Hölderlin, for example. Third, they talk about greening nature by quoting from poems and stories. Fourth, they listen to the weather report, in which green plays a role and flashes into mind for them as a colour. Fifth, they see the green in satellite photos and are enchanted.

151
I see satellite photos of the Alps online. I zoom in to the Schafkopf and other chunks of rock, to give me an idea of what they look like.

152
Shortly after cancelling I came down with a fever, which knocked me out for two days; it was not because of my suspicious mind, not mountain fever in the negative sense. It was a virus, a stomach bug that struck not just me.

153
After the fever days I ended up in Reckenbühlstrasse in Lucerne, at the invitation of Ruth's friends, who were travelling, and even if they hadn't been travelling they'd have taken me in for as long as I liked, they said.
Ruth makes contact connections (super-spreading), introduces people to each other and watches how the introducees then fare.

154
In a fully furnished second-floor guest apartment with a view of the Pilatus, I am at a safe distance from the mountains, in the close vicinity of the city and in possession of sufficient space to spread out my notes on the floor.

155
Now that most of the notes are spread flat, I can see the problems with my parallel diaries. I can put the topics relating to colours into one folder, but then there are other mountain topics alongside the mountain colours, and when it comes to skin colours they're to do with people, while people go in with the portraits; the incongruity within the groupings leads me down a dead end.

156
There will not be ten or twelve themed diaries. I am standing at the window looking out on the city. I went out with the dog earlier and now I shall stay by the window a while.

157
There are heaps of diaries; those heaps inevitably start slipping and sliding apart. What goes in a standard diary in

the first place? I for one would never write about my daily digestion.

158

Either I keep all the hotel guests I have met in the folder with the portraits, or they go in the hotel collection.

I am repeating myself; it is my self-echo. Working primarily on mountains, I cannot avoid reverberations.

One solution might be to put all my notes together and mix up the heap, the way playing cards are shuffled.

159

Ten pictures of three persons, eleven of two persons, two of four persons, one of a single person. A total of twenty-four portraits, all taken at the top cable-car station.

160

Flash photo in Leukerbad. The blonde at the next table, a young woman, could hardly hold her coffee cup; her arms trembled from wrist to elbow.

161

The restaurant owner, well over forty and very laid-back, paused at each table with her hips slanted forwards. A nice relaxed stance. Her home-baked bread was a big hit, another source of her confidence, and when she spoke to a woman she paused up close to her in that connective stance with her hips inclined forwards. For women, this physical closeness happens mainly when they are young. They embrace one another or grab a bite from each other's plate.

162
Among the sheets of paper on the floor, I found a scrap with two words on it. Monotonous and trudge. There is a story perched in those two words: three women walking along a path single file, me sitting on a bench watching the women's heavy strides, their steady trudge and stern wordlessness.

163
The newcomers in the mountains are not keen on steep slopes and bold adventures. They refuse them at first, and perhaps later too. They find the countless flags oppressive, flags everywhere, marked-out territories.

The group leaders want to take action. There are too many fainthearted hesitators, too many failed attempts, they proclaim. All it takes on the slopes is a firm step and then any old exotic fowl can fly high, they say.

164
A woman fell while on a hike in Ticino. Her two children and her husband could do nothing but watch, simply watch. A misstep, then the fall. She was an experienced mountain climber but that did not protect her.

165
The speed of her fall is sure to have played a part. The falling woman's velocity. The acceleration during her fall.

166
It later emerged that the teenager wanted to strangle his cousin. Religious mania. He felt better on Sundays. In safe hands, he said to himself, and he laid both his

hands on the dinner table. Once a month, always on a Sunday, he felt better.

167
Everyone is a suspect. They have not done anything yet. The only strange thing is their tone of voice; they sound over-excited. A conspiracy is suspected in the background, and the suspects are dirty, dishonest, unnatural, devious, exaggerated, concentrated in conversation only on their own intent, and now they cajole the main character into jumping from the world's tallest building.

168
The detectives tell the relatives 'I understand,' and the answer is usually 'You don't understand anything.' That is understandable, the situation makes sense. A person is in the depths of grief, the detective wants to help but the shattered father or the beautiful mother is inconsolable. In fact, it is the inconsolability that is shattering, so a well-meaning detective is no help at all. He can only justify his work once he finds the murderer.

169
I read in a remarkable book that a crime story only begins with a corpse.

170
Crime shows are all about how no one wants to accept someone dying. Dying is hokum. First a person exists, and then they don't. Elephants, pigeons and other species are equally disturbed by this upheaval. What the detective is supposed to help with is actually the vanishing. In crime

shows, however, the criminal takes centre stage.

171
What use is a murderer who doesn't kill! Suddenly no one dies any more. The elephants go crazy and dig up the mammoths.

172
A hit-and-run on the highway; a woman sustains life-threatening injuries. The police soon show up. The transplanters turn up immediately too, saving first the heart, still beating, then the healthy lung and the liver, which turns out later to be no good, tough luck. Before the detectives can reach their conclusions, the other organs are whisked off by copter to the designated clinic. The two plain-clothes investigators, a man and a woman, pay a call on the widower, who knows nothing of the events, and they say that his wife's heart, a last remnant of the accident, will soon be beating in a cardiac patient's body. The widower breaks down, his brain unusable because he understood nothing in the moment of his death, refusing to understand, but his liver is fine. A funeral follows with empty corpses.

CID are wary of passing the case on to the financial crimes department, which might convict the beneficiaries (pharmaceutical industry, medics) for their profiteering, but then a newly founded department enters the fray. Interpol against medical attempts at rejigging the conscience.

173
Ancient Egyptian immortalisations. Thorough cleansing of the body, removal of the brain and the innards, which

are preserved separately. High esteem for the body through embalming. Contrast against our exchangeable organs, like modules these days.

174
And yet at the same time they have introduced ID cards with precise fingerprints, and soon the precise position of our eyes will be key. I must be recognisable for my ID cards, while for the life that shall never end, I can incorporate others into myself.

175
A manhunt. It is hard to tell the difference between disingenuous and desolate. Aside from that, there are stories that are swallowed up by other stories.

176
With three rescue missions in a matter of hours, the junior doctor from Thailand had plenty on her plate. She was very brave, I said. It was all fine by her, she replied, it makes the day pass quicker.

177
I nudge the door open, inching into the house with my left shoulder forward, clutching my gun at chest level and pivoting on my own axis; now I take another step, right shoulder forward, look around, shout Police, another step with my left shoulder forward, keeping my back to a wall wherever I can, Police, I shout, holding my gun at chest level, take another step, hold my breath, say nothing, and now I am not with the police but on the other side, feeling my way with my right shoulder, there's a policeman facing

me, Put your gun down and your hands up, he shouts, I put the gun down, put my hands up, he comes closer, and then I whip out a second gun from my jacket pocket and he shoots me in the leg, or in fact I am the policeman; I kneel down, put the gun on the floor; my opponent, a possible criminal, is not agitated and neither am I but we are breathing vehemently; the backup team moves in outside, around forty people who would hardly move in spontaneously – from where and with what kind of warrant could they ever be drummed up so quickly? – but they move in, leaning forward with their knees slightly bent as they tread quietly closer and surround the house, wearing visors in front of their faces; I kneel, not looking at the rifle facing me, try to see my opponent's eyes and think of the people marching in, I think that I'm in a movie, and as I'm thinking about the movie, my opponent notices the backup team and runs away.

178
Criminalistics of archaeology: there are mountain ranges, mountain chains, mountain ridges. When did what happen? Isolated thrusts from the earth's core while the tectonic plates were shifting. First the Dachstein was shoved up and up, then, with the next hefty thrust, Mont Blanc – or vice versa. First Mont Blanc, then the Dachstein.

179
The young Alps in the morning light. A tableau of the Alps. The burden the mountain ranges bear. The pressure of the rock.

High German for an incubus or a succubus haunting our

dreams: Alpdruck, elves pressing on our chests, Alpine pressure. These days, a nightmare is an Alptraum, an Alpine dream. Thankfully, we cannot cultivate more mountains.

180
It's best for everyone to learn all the Alpine passes by heart. They add up to an education; though it's clear that many don't know how the passes were formed. The Albula Pass was created artificially, by an explosion. I found a photo of the pass on the internet. Not far from a resolute mountain house stands a cow, a single cow on the sparse grass.

181
Many peaks in the Alps are self-similar. I picked up self-similarity on a TV show; they also talked about fractal geometry. Using fractals enables us to calculate the shape of the mountains including their peaks, an architect explained on the show. We can imagine fractals like Persian fabric patterns or images that come about inside a kaleidoscope. The mountain formations came about quasi-inside a kaleidoscope.

182
It was an architect talking about fractals on the show, and about mountain formations. Sam is an architect and there was the gigantic architect in Venice with his diaries, and whether they have anything in common beyond their profession is uncertain. Sam's most recent statement about the Alps was that he would cement several mountains together, using a tried-and-trusted Roman cement mix. Black, if possible, he said. He meant he'd do it off the books.

183
I first learnt about the Alps in books. Mossy green slopes and forests, an eagle soaring high above, looking down on a vast stretch. Good green, the silence and the eagle. I was not yet of age when I read that. Now, on second reading, I have found that memorable passage in Hofmannsthal's unfinished novel (*Andreas oder die Vereinigten*), two short pages with the eagle and the green, but otherwise I am disappointed by the rather contrived story. Only a few moments jut out, but those that do I take with me, along with the eagle (or the eagle quote), whenever I am in the mountains.

184
Later, I wandered the Alps with Goethe. A group of heavily laden donkeys passed along high bridle tracks to isolated buildings, to friendly, orderly people. Up there, the cotton they delivered was spun in living rooms and thence transported to lower regions, again on the heavily loaded beasts of burden. Down there, the weaving was done.

185
When I'm in the car, when I'm on a train – I look up, see the mountain walls and know that the spinners and the weavers (the spinsters and the websters) were displaced by fast machines into the valleys, down to the vales or to America. That was how the uncomfortable mountain regions were depopulated, and Goethe's ecological and economic description of his times shows his prescience. Goethe On the Road.

186
I could tear my hair out (I must look after my hair) when

works considered classics are pushed out of reach by that very classification. So let it be with Goethe.

As classics, they are at the peak, high up in the distance, so even if that man On the Road had his eye on the market economy from the outset, it hardly helps him much.

Manu says I shouldn't get het up, and she photographs the face I have pulled.

187
No one really likes the peaks; they climb them to combat them.

188
On one of his journeys Goethe spent the night in Altdorf, and in the hotel he noted that people in the Swiss mountains do not aufdrücken a door to open it, but aufstossen it. The door has to be gestossen, not gedrückt – thrust, not pushed.

189
A friend wrote to me recently that his daughter, giving birth to her baby, had to drück for a good while, whereas I am of the opinion that she had to press, not drück. Certainly not stoss. This note goes with the language portraits.

190
Language portraits. Mirror, mirror, on the wall.

191
Goethe writes in *Wilhelm Meister* that the spinsters sang

psalms, and the websters sang hymns. Another interesting observation.

192
For Goethe, stossen was a kind of written sound recording. I presume he had travelling companions who made it easier for him to talk to people in the Alps and noted down particular words for him. He would barely have understood the Swiss mountain German, and he listened less to the sound of the language than to particular unfamiliar (unsettling) terms. These days, I have other minor objections to his Alpine passage; but his spinners and weavers and their connection to industrialisation are still part of my own mountain observations.

193
How shall I deal with the mountain ranges I have seen for myself, and how with the other mountains, which I only know from pictures or films or of which I have heard or read, or which I have only imagined! Do I place them side by side, do I push them together, or shall I store them separately? I could check with my eyes closed which of them seem more vivid.

194
There are trees in the landscape that one sees in the moment, and then there are photos and filmed trees, trees from one's own past, novel-trees where lovers linger, fear-trees, dark gallows-trees.

195
There is an immense trove of forgetfulnesses; these

forgetfulnesses are a vast, untilled field, and in that field stand people, each with a hole in their brain; we talk to them, the six of us talk to those with a hole in their brain, and each of us has our own hole. We do not know the name of the man we are talking to, whom we have seen several times before.

196
My memories becloud, bedim, blur, shine blurrily forth, grow steady again.

197
A boy was jumping around between the rocks and then noticed us, saw Manu and me, watched us attentively for a while, his round eyes focused mainly on Manu; she smiled, he smiled back tentatively and then ran away.

198
Above him the azure sky. I say that because I did not make any notes about the sky and clouds along the way, although I know that clouds are not romantic constructs but are to do with topography, with the wind, humidity and the relative temperatures. Precise observations would be worthwhile. I ought to ask Lucius. I could call him but then we'd end up in a rambling conversation, so I put off the call until another time.

Recently, he said that he was not a mountain functionary; at best a mountain weather situation functionary. Laughing, he wanted to invite Manu and me to visit a cave. How little he knows us! He would have a great deal to say about clouds, though.

199
Unexpectedly, he turned up at Reckenbühlstrasse with Ruth to take me out for lunch; he wanted to go to La Corona on Lake Walen. He had taken the whole day off, and Ruth would have made up the missing time at the office later, but the trip seemed too long to me. A good hour to get there and then the return journey, while I wanted to savour the silence in the guest apartment, so we just popped out to the Eichhof Brewery restaurant and I got a good barley broth there.

200
Manu sent me photos of eight people, by email. Silhouettes, differing figures on a mountain ridge. They were people who had been herded up there, she wrote. Later we talked via Skype and Manu's even face looked as though I were viewing her through a poor-quality magnifying glass.

201
Almost all my protagonists are tall. Manu is 180 centimetres tall, for instance, Sam 185, the weather narrator a tad taller, and I would say the diary writer in Venice, at more than 190 centimetres, would top them all. Then again, Ruth comes across as rather small and delicate.

202
While I was looking for the bus stop in Engadin, a man came towards me. A mountain man born and bred. His steps did not come from the hip; instead, he placed one leg in front of the other. A leggy gait. You want to go to St Moritz, he asked, lowering his head so as not to look me in the eye. But his question was friendly.

203
Four men in a sunny square of fog, part of the Bernina vaguely visible behind them. The men are waving, their ascent still ahead of them.

204
The Bernina is made up of three peaks, so they say, which I cannot follow since I see at least ten points in all depictions. I probably don't quite understand how peaks are defined.

205
There was once a blossoming meadow on the Bernina, so they say, a high pasture owned by a man known far and wide as a pinchfist. To punish him, a large part of the mountain land froze over. The new punishment is that the glaciers are melting.

206
Cave painters were out and about again. They entered a tunnel together, all three of them in neon-green vests. They wrote animal names on the wall of one of the caves in oversized letters: eagle, hedgehog, wolf, dog, donkey, ibex and others. Later they said there was nothing as consistent as cave painting.

207
A wild animal drawn blood-red / a wild mammoth, an antelope / a wild deer, something deer-like / on the run, then three men / striding, seen side-on / all in ochre.

208
Recently, Lake Sils in Engadin a dark, matt turquoise,

beyond it the salmon-coloured front of a small bar. A guest in the bar talked about skin-coloured fabrics.

209
Without sun, the cliffs on the eastern shore of Lake Uri are grey-white, and grey-white and white are both colours.

All is calm, all is bright. Later the cliffs receive a little sun, and from then on they are greenish and blue-grey, white in some places. All in all, the mountain flanks have a range of restrained colours.

210
Vivid pale brown next to umber or black. Matt grey beside deep dark blue. A light earth brown, beautiful next to black or dark green. Mountain air and Alpine air can be substituted for indigo. The sky is temporarily white, extremely pale. Towards evening the silhouettes of the mountain ranges are almost black, neither dark grey nor dark brown but almost black, the multitude of grey areas remarkable; I could talk about the grey-rich Alps and skip the green on the lower levels. Orange is not present. I should emphasise the shades of grey as a record of the colours. I have not mentioned turquoise. A comparable colour is mined inside the mountains, as emerald. A little emerald trickles out of the Alps via the rivers, all the way down to the Danube.

211
Then there are mountain crystals, their colours a challenge, thus forming a parallel to diamonds. Forming is a good word, especially with reference to colours.

212
Almost monochrome; more monochromatic the closer you get to the border. Dun would be the right word. The closer the border gets, the more dun. Yet another border. Everyone must stop, descend into dun silence and then undress slowly in all modesty. First shoes are removed, then outer clothing, then underclothes and finally inner clothing. Those crossing the border and stopped for the first time are allowed to dress again immediately after a brief inspection, and sometimes the undressing and redressing takes place so quickly that barely anyone notices the procedure, comparable to the split-second advertisements of American movie legend. Only once you breathe a sigh, on the other side of the border, do you notice how colourless the story is.

213
Sam wrote to me that he would compile a list of all subjects and problems he wants to exclude from his notes; Sam is constantly noting down his thoughts, more than me, and we rarely show each other our respective entries, but I am curious to see his list of unmentioned things.

214
Travellers include sportspeople, holidaymakers, sales representatives with business dealings abroad, exchange students, smugglers, voluntary and involuntary courtesans, agents, members of parliament, celebrity chefs, geologists and a large number of photographers, which I have mentioned previously (there goes my self-echo), because I often think of these itinerants and also about the backgrounds to their expeditions. The backgrounds tell us a great deal, and the first question is why a person is travelling.

In the midst of this tumult comes a sudden order to stop; everyone is compelled to stop still wherever they are, trapped, so that they gradually become residents, all involuntarily, achieving a vague equality. All are made equal, temporarily.

A while passes, no one moves, all that happens is that some wonder where they have ended up. They look around, gradually trying to get their bearings because to begin with they were frozen, listless even towards themselves, they were frozen in place at the start, and depending on their own backstories, most of them were more dulled than excited. They were out of it. Their heads were switched off, granting protection in shock situations. There follows the recovery phase, everyone thaws out again, and as time passes they begin telling of the exceptional state they have experienced. They tell of how they were prevented from moving on and were trapped, describing their spectral situation; some feel comfortable in their misfortune; at any rate they hunch over their notes simultaneously, not seeing one another, all writing alone and simultaneously, and that has a touch of indecency to it.

215

Which brings me back to the problematic keyword diary and the architect, who has no doubt since increased the number of his separate notes even more, while I have almost only empty folders on my desk. There is not a single note in the folder labelled Nations, Various Countries. Nations, for goodness' sake! And I have entirely given up on precisely separating the inseparable topics.

216
Sam is continuing his sound recordings in London, in the lowlands there, as he says. He has been to markets to record material, to covered markets, and in favourable weather he has sat down for a coffee outside cafés, in al fresco cafés, as he says, and placed his recorder on the table. He played me a few samples on a trip home. We were on the street outside Manu's shop when Milly, his ex, came up to him and embraced him. Why was he neither in London nor in Basel nor at his office, she asked, but she didn't need an answer. He hummed something to her and rocked her a little, his ex, who then put both her hands in mine and quickly moved on. Later I heard from Manu that Milly had a photo appointment with her and they wanted to talk about fabric samples.

217
A year ago, at a festival with two or three hundred people between benches and tables, I felt instantaneously anxious. I have bad memories of large gatherings.

218
Hundreds lining the street, forming a swarm. Many women are among them, including older women wearing make-up, and they're crying. To be precise, they're sobbing, hundreds sobbing; many have previously laid bouquets while the others queue patiently to lay their flowers and tea lights. One of the men says he has never cried like this before.

219
Thousands lining the streets and unafraid to be in their thousands. Swarm formation. Suddenly they burst into

tears; the media has its guts in a twist. They all lay flowers, cry, throw stones, survive and can talk to nobody.

220
Scholars offer contradictory statements about the Neanderthals; hence, the question remains unresolved as to whether they lived in smaller groups than *Homo sapiens*, who have always tolerated or even preferred a community of hundreds. The Neanderthal groups consisted of thirty people at most, and I appear to have a significant proportion of genes from them, being gripped by fear at all larger gatherings.

221
We have known for some time that everyone whose ancestors were from the northern hemisphere displays a minimal percentage of Neanderthal, and the people from whom these minimal percentages originate were also in the Alps. In groups of thirty, they roamed the mountains and knew both Alpdruck and Alptraum.

222
Reckenbühlstrasse, hikes around Lucerne with the dog, breaks in between at a café where tourists prefer to pass by without entering, but are clearly visible. Swarm formation in smaller groups, thousands roaming the city in all, but in each case about thirty people, groups of Neanderthals. Along comes a sudden order to stop, and they all run back to their buses, embark, fly back home, and then tourism becomes extinct like the mammoths once did, and the people of Lucerne and the rest of the Alps starve to death.

223
Quiet time in the guest apartment. There were two of us in Reckenbühlstrasse for a few days, and then Sam called us the couple with the dog. Here comes the couple with the dog, he said, or he asked whether he should bring ice cream for the couple with the dog.

224
I have started a new folder for illnesses, but Sam, who throws away his own notes, says he will design a wooden house for me instead of the folders, with rooms opening into one another back to back where I could store everything I disparagingly call my diary, and then I would have walkable spaces. For the content of the folders, I would have a circuit to tour, and I could show the various records or contents in display cases. We could close the door on the not yet clearly defined rooms – he showed me how we could close it – and hang a sign on the door saying Building Site.

225
I shall go to the mountains again soon with Manu, to a quarry near the Via Mala where the Alptraum is mined, the Alpdruck, the burdensome dream on the mountains. There must be people for whom the Alps stack up to marble and good stone and who think of renowned sculptors, not ski slopes, says Manu. Quarries in the mountains on one side, ski slopes on the other.

226
A mountain family, five individuals, a small group on an Alp. They need no one; quite the opposite: they avoid

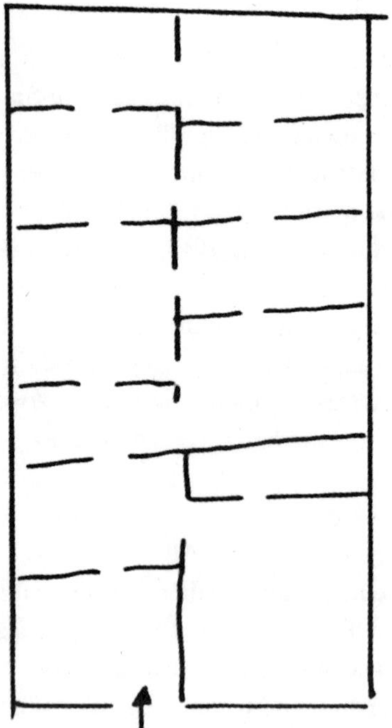

close contact. They say they don't want to quarrel, never want to complain, and yet they quarrel and complain all the more; a fine five-character tragedy. That's what they like because it's what they are used to, and they do not want to go without their assets, their habits, for heaven's sake.

227

A campaign was held in spring in a former tannery, courses for hikers focused not on practical exercises but on a lecture by an expert. He would not deny, he said, that dangers lay in wait in some mountain areas, but there was no need for qualms – only respect. He spoke slowly, his tone always resonant, his words resonating, and to achieve this sombre sound he inserted a series of pauses, even mid-sentence.

228

Practice, training, drill, to get to like the Matterhorn. Exposure to the mountain is a purely therapeutic exercise. Close your eyes and listen for a possible echo. The idea is not to turn away heartlessly from the Matterhorn. If those in training still dislike the mountain after the exercise, they will be out of pocket, time wasted, but first of all they should expose themselves to it. They should close their eyes in the face of the big white mountain horn that they do not wish to climb, and develop a feeling for the innards of the mountain. On the inside of this rough hulk there are minerals. They should take no notice of the people arrived from abroad and standing alongside them, looking up at the horn and exclaiming, Oh wonderful. These travellers had adjusted to the circumstances before they travelled, force-fed Wonderful and unable to see for real. They think the white horn is called Wonderful. The real practitioners, however, want to overcome their heartlessness; their practice means turning to face the mountain, turning to face it is all a matter of practice, and then they will manage the first step. They wonder how long this hulk might have been there. The rest remains open.

229

I am more of an observer of mountain silhouettes.

230

At a height of two thousand metres, we were set down by a helicopter on the ground outside the hut. I wanted to try out the altitude up there and savour the altitudinous view without having to climb, and an unexpected bonus payment meant I could afford the excursion. We were to be picked up again the next day.

Undertakings of this kind rely on good contacts or financial reserves, and I have limited admiration for such excursions. In addition, I consider travellers colonists, and that meant I too was occupying the hut at two thousand metres.

There was a barley broth in the early evening, even better than the first one I'd eaten in Chur, and a good chunk of cheese as well, but the warden informed us with clenched teeth that a storm warning had been issued the night before. He himself had originally wanted to fly away in the helicopter that had brought us, so as not to experience the predicted stormy night, but no one had listened to him, as if he were a mountain vole. So es G'heu: what rot. And now we have the storm to look forward to. Don't be afraid, he said, it might be fine.

Later, the gusts blew open a window – aufgestossen, the hut warden said – shattered the panes. Our host came with boards and nailed up the gap. Then came more shattering.

231
In another mountain lodge, I had my own room. No one forced me to the edge of the steep slope, I did not have to look down to the depths from the harsh incline, and after two days I knew which mountain to expect the morning sun to appear behind. It would have been best to stretch out on a deck chair by the wall of the building and stare out at nothing.

232
I took the mountain railway up to the hotel, then sat at a table with a stranger who regaled me uninterrupted with stories about his past, mountain affairs, political affairs, love affairs. He sprayed his cheating right in my face. After dinner, I got up, wanting to be alone, but he followed me and regaled me with more episodes from his invented life. I like the quiet in the mountains, I told him, but still he went on talking, and this dissonance made me feel genuinely nauseous, which is down to an ancient disease, not a hereditary disease but an ur-disease I have contracted of my own accord, but which I stand by.

233
What happens when six people are trapped in the mountains and are overcome by an icy storm. Will they die? What do they say as the storm comes in and the cabin cannot stand up to it?

234
The six people are carried to their graves.

235
Indigo could be substituted for mountain air and Alpine air, so I have breathed in indigo.

236
We arrived at the hotel delayed, which they took as an affront to begin with, but later they let us order a little something to eat in the restaurant. Outside we saw mountain silhouettes and, at a certain distance, lights, the lighting of other mountain restaurants.

237
The memories of the separate mountaintops peek out of the sea of fog; or memories, some of them, are located above the fog. Perhaps I could use the topographical term shoulder drop in this context, referring to what is visible beyond the fog.

238
A sad chapter. Drop. Descend, dive, dip. Plummet, hurtle, tumble, plunge. Then skids, scratches, scrapes and scuffs.

239
On the way down from the rocky heights, trees soon came into play, then railway tracks, a train incarnate passed us by, and from the cable car a village gradually grew visible in the valley.

240

The fact that the dog enjoys flying with us is another incentive for theoretical flight plans, for flights that are out of the question. The losers of all this flying are clear (the mountains only one of them); the consequences are not worth discussing.

From Lucerne it takes a good hour to Mont Ventoux. The giant stands illuminated in the west, and illuminated in the east stands the Dachstein, even further east the Vienna Woods with their slopes down to the Danube, and when I speak of west and east, I see myself in the middle.

A number of watersheds, water divides can be seen or guessed at from above, and sometimes even weather divides.

Since I like flying but refuse to fly, I am allowed to imagine the ideal flight altitude and picture the weather situation.

We are silent during the flight, looking down on the Alps, looking into the valleys.

Love of flying is embedded in our bones and might explain our urgent lust for overview.

The dog cannot smell the ground from a plane, he can hear nothing remarkable over the noise of the engine, he relies on his not particularly strong eyesight, so on his previous flights he concentrated on his sight. And on boat trips, he quickly grew accustomed to the speed and the field of vision.

241
Before the planned trip to the Schafkopf, I went to Uri for a second time and stayed with Herr Epp, the warden of the mountain lodge. I was in a fairly familiar place, although it was only a small portion of familiarity, a room where I could look out into the surroundings from the protection of a large desk and enjoy a day without having to listen to talk of swings, and swings to the right.

My host welcomed me with a sparse smile. Later I understood that he had found an injured sparrowhawk that morning, in the woods lower down the slope. A large female, she had had trouble breathing and had grown apathetic, he told me (if I understood rightly). He had taken the sparrowhawk into his home and briefly hoped for recovery, but at noon he had to lay the dead bird on a rock away from the house, so that at least the other birds could make use of its corpse. Now the bird was in sparrowhawk heaven, he said.

242
There is a sparrowhawk heaven, a heaven for mountain eagles, a sheep heaven, one for Alpine choughs and one for wolves; there is a heavenly cartography for one and all.

243
This time it rained incessantly on the mountain and there was no need to observe the clouds. I had planned notes on beetles and flies, on all the beetles I have ever crushed under my feet and all the flies that have sought me out in their hour of death. I was going to add an extremely detailed description of the spider I had observed for several days on a window. Her web was large and pedantically beautiful

and always apparently empty, since she stayed hidden behind the window frame on the outside of the window, but as soon as a fly ended up in her web she raced across the threads on her black-and-white-striped legs to her prey. First the disciplined attention, then the sprint, and once she had sprung her trap she stayed with the fly and held it in a long, firm embrace. That calm after springing the trap was what I wanted to describe.

244
In the afternoon Herr Epp summoned his guests for coffee. A young Swedish couple was among us, staying in the room next to mine, and they sat closely side by side in the kitchen. We stuttered friendly yeses and nos, nodded and ate pastries, then a man joined us unexpectedly. He happened to be in the area, he said.

How can anyone happen to be in this isolated area by chance!

The visitor was pre-programmed, a pre-programmed man with an unmoving expression and a freshly ironed shirt (he was roaming the area in a freshly ironed shirt); he talked about his health, he was an advocate of health, he said, and regaled us with his morning routine, told us he breathed in and out by an open window every day. The Swedish couple left the room quietly, and when I too wanted to leave the warden drummed his fingers on the tabletop, which the visitor could hardly have missed – but he went on regaling. Our host barely looked at him and the guest stared right past him as well.

245
Without much thought, I could place other people alongside this visitor, all of them around the same height, wiry and determinedly self-satisfied, and I could mix all four of them up.

246
How different individuals take a seat at a table, how they sit, which questions they ask, which they never ask, how these people ignore questions, how they don't look at the people they are apparently addressing when they talk – they stare into a corner or into the distance. A group portrait with a basic pattern.

247
I thought from the outset that the warden had a southern touch to him; it was not his measured motions, not his language, but perhaps it was his calm, sonorous voice. Let's say Epp's father had fallen for an Italian woman, or it was his great-grandfather, or both the great-grandfather and the father had fallen for Italian women. The Epps of Uri loved women who had crossed the Alps from the south. When the Gotthard Tunnel was built. But it was mostly men who came from Italy to build the Gotthard Tunnel, and their names were not Epp.

Does asking these questions about the history of a certain person help me to get to know the person better? If it is about only their origins, I must rule out the thought from the outset; I want nothing to do with those questions about origins and ancestors.

248
A storm would follow on immediately from the rainy period, Lucius had informed me by text message, and yet I had still not expected a storm after the incessant rain. I thought turbulence was linked to extreme weather changes, dry versus wet, hot versus cold, but then a fully fledged thunderstorm came over us, with great gusts of wind. Power lines were torn down, railway tracks blocked by fallen trees. The trees were forced to fall.

249
It was only after the storm that I saw how empty the villages were. I was in a badly lit dining area somewhere in no man's land, sitting beside unoccupied tables. Later I saw red kites hunting outside, but barely any people. Beside the little inn stood two damply gleaming horses, their heads lowered. They trotted slowly towards me.

250
They say Glenn Gould loved talking to animals most of all. So do I, especially to tapirs.

251
Aboard the postbus to Hertenstein, I saw an establishment with the blue-illuminated name of Club B, and next door to it a hairdresser by the name of Lockenstube: curl parlour. Inventive names – that is the new poetry. I got off the bus and went into Club B, where I drank a hot coffee alongside teens with their backs turned to the television.

252
A documentary about Mont Blanc covered what is known

as water pockets, running water underneath glaciers, which normally takes decades to trickle from the peak to the foot of the thick ice sheets. But when the glacier melts too fast, the rising water bursts through the cavities, breaks through the surface of the glacier and the gigantic slope is flooded, all the way down to the valley. In the nineteenth century, one of the first groups of tourists was killed in such a flood.

253

Frozen corpses. Corpses in the mountains, one in Scandinavia, one in the Alps, both frozen over. A female person, found recently, stares endlessly up at the sky, it seems, although she no longer has eyes.

254

Are frozen ice-corpse women friendly? They say women are well disposed to one another, but such generalised friendliness would be a joke few women find funny.

255

In practically every village, even the main roads are empty. When a bus stops at its usual interval, two or three people disembark and immediately disappear. Empty pavements, no car horns, though no one has been locked in or locked away. The silence is a sign of digital labour. Everyone can be reached by internet, no one need set foot in the street. Outside a front door a young couple are intensely entangled, which is hardly heroic and would not be so in a busy area, either, except now the two of them have no need to think, since no one will see them.

256
Love no longer occurs, abolished since Darwin; what remains is diaries and calendars with brief notes.

257
Just now, I lost another second's thought, even though I find these short sprinklings of ideas useful to capture the details of a moment.

258
Mobile phone photos in the Alps are also interested in the moment.

Experiences are deposited by photo and only experienced later.

The photos created don't count as experiences, for the time being, because taking snapshots requires only short bursts of concentration, Manu says, and Ruth laughs because she agrees.

259
Transient ideas and the Alps are closely related. In both cases, a person needs surefootedness. One false move during mental mountaineering and the thought plummets.

260
Surly, dismissive, hostile, wordless, impassive, disdainful, impersonal.

Digital silences, altered forms of politeness. No responses to the simplest of questions. Whatever you do, do not respond! Many people are so busy that they really cannot respond, while the ones who do respond probably have a lot of time because they're not needed.

261
If you have time, go to the mountains. If you can't get the hang of the mountains, turn around and go home. That would be the mountain-lovers' view. There is this view and that view. From my perspective is not a bad phrase. This tolerant formulation has snuck in recently; it usually appears in commentaries on sporting competitions, and competitions are certainly relevant in the Alps. The Alps are a sports ground. From my perspective they are a sports facility.

When did Alpine admiration come about!

262
I shall draw a steep slope that can only be conquered in climbing shoes. On the way up, my well-trained arm muscles, leg muscles, abdominal muscles are visible, my focused gaze trained on the mountain, but I slip and fall.

263
There are my-mountains and not-my-mountains, but after this calming insight we return to the digital; in part it is useful, in part too much silence arises and we lack direct contact. One compensation is swarm formation. Thousands come together. They cannot yet compete with the surprising formations of starlings, the flight manoeuvres of their huge black flocks.

264

Other than that, the silence remains. On Lake Walen I go into a bakery, stand there alone, see various pastries for warming up on display and the necessary microwave at the back, and I do not say that I would like a slice of spinach quiche but instead I use the local term Spinatwähe; but I am not understood, my pronunciation gets in the way. A tourist trying too hard to please, the baker thinks, not hiding his thoughts, and he smiles the way people smile at strangers who are welcome to pass through. I'm not a tourist, I say, and I point my finger at the slice I want him to warm up for me. What does he know about pronunciation! He doesn't want to know much about it; he has a vague idea of how the Grisons speak, accepts the Glarners, the respected Berners, he knows his way more or less around the central Alpine region, hears the differences instantly – though he doesn't find the Appenzellers' accent attractive – but there are limits to his tolerance. The unpleasantly unfamiliar begins in Austria and Germany, that's when his ears close up. The ears protect themselves, especially in mountain landscapes. Every valley has its own tone. (Every family has its own tone; I'm repeating myself, there's my echo again.)

While my quiche is heating up I look out at the Kurfürsten across the lake, and the baker is glad to see me leaving his shop.

265

Navigating the southern shore of Lake Walen must have been an effort in the past; now it is simple enough and the view of the lake and over to the northern shore is inviting: a few groups of houses cluster at the foot of the Kurfürsten. The Kurfürsten are ennobled mountains; the Fürsten in their name makes princes of them. The houses at their feet can only be reached by boat. A description fit for a travel brochure.

266
We are going into advertising, looking for a suitable job, Manu and I. We are going into advertising so as not to keep putting up resistance. We will go along with everything.

267
How can we capitalise on the mountains? Marble and other high-quality stone would be one opportunity, and another offer would be adoration of the mountains. We shall therefore switch modes and do something to advertise tourism. We shall begin in Engadin, because even they are short of visitors. I shall therefore write an advertising diary, or at least a number of slogans.

268
In many mountain shapes, one of the two short sides (if we can speak of short sides) is rounded and the back is craggy, declining vertically. I ought to start at an advertising agency with the simplified explanation that the famous Mont Blanc has several different sides, as do Säntis and the bare, chalk-white Mont Ventoux. On one side, Mont Blanc is steep, on the other almost mellow. Tourists' attention should be directed at the multi-sidedness of mountain shapes.

269
Especially for hiking groups, this attention to mountain shapes would effect a deceleration. Instead of constantly focusing on their next step, they would stop more to look around.

270

Would we provide copy, photos and drawings for our advertising? Or would we prefer to be tour guides and drive around the landscape in buses with thirty participants at most, taking special notice of rivers, streams and lakes? The Alps and their water. We could emphasise the subject of water. Cave waters, waterfalls, fog, snow, old and newer ice masses, water seeping into the rail and road tunnels. Shall we bring Lucius in for the cavities in the beautiful rock faces, so he can mention the old military camps and bunkers inside the mountains? Or describe the typical cloud formations of the Alps? We could connect several matters, latch them together or separate the themes.

271

Our guests may stalk, stomp, stumble, stroll, stand. Gaits according to the ground, according to the stoniness of the stock.

272

We would begin in Engadin, be friendly to the arrivals and never bluff, we would never cheat them, we would certainly talk of the hollowed-out mountains, of the less edifying aspects, but we would also remind them of the cave paintings, of paintings in general. Every mountain shape could be sketched a hundred times over, depending on the light. And then we'd come back to the caves and the grottoes and other places of shelter. The hollow inside spaces in the Alps are brimming with internal stories, and we would tell them and later take a break together over air-dried ham and cheese.

273
Our little tourist groups have hard-wearing legs, even when standing still. As they listen to us, some of them think of their ancestors' earlier travels, the famous Grand Tours to Italy, the explorations of Greece, and they think of the women who once ventured halfway across Africa. Even earlier than that there was the Odyssey; now you can do your own Odyssey trip in a day, and cameramen and camerawomen are currently capturing insights into the curated loneliness of their travels so that their audiences have no need to travel themselves.

274
Watching the cameramen's and camerawomen's films, audiences do not experience changes in the air, they are not in the surroundings that they see, they cannot perceive any particular smells (I ought to add that in German-speaking Switzerland, in the mountains and valleys of German-speaking Switzerland, there is no separate verb for smelling, they use only the verb for tasting: schmecken; the nose does the tasting as well as the smelling – it all smacks of noses – which is not incorrect, anatomically, and from that point of view it is correct that the audience cannot taste anything in the filmic surroundings either).

275
We shall take one of our groups to a festival where forty or fifty artists appear alongside each other in the space of a few hours, and the organisers play the main role. The organisers are a sign of the times, buying in artists in bulk – but that distracts from their intense though slim performances. The organisers have the right budget to attract the

media. You can imagine the media people – thankfully not all of them – stumbling after them, slithering towards them. Where else are they to go? Sparkling wine and other drinks are served after the events, thanks to the sponsors.

276
At one such reception, our little group with their hard-wearing legs stood at the tall round tables, all drinking bubbly and looking around. Afterwards we asked them what they thought of the event. They gave us a friendly smile.

277
We are in Engadin, in a natural exhibition room in the high Inn Valley, in the land of the classic painters. Prestigious people have passed through. That is a useful statement. And to a certain extent we are in the land of the Danube's origins, because the Inn, which will become the Large Inn, flows into the Danube.

278
I am a mountain silhouette observer and I also like to see the entirety of the Alps from above, rather like in an atlas, like on a topographic map, but I would have to climb up to the height of the satellites to get that kind of view. From up there, I would zoom in on Engadin until I spot Manu and her tourist group. As always, she's wearing something matt green, sand green; she is showing her people something high up and then she points up at me, and because her audience is from German-speaking Switzerland she's speaking Lucerne German.

279
In the back office, Sam collects phrases on his voice recorder that cannot be said. For example, Alpine antiquity. The Alps in antiquity, however, does make sense.

As an example, he has recorded phrases about the railway station in Brig, which he found on the internet. Pizza and kebab bistro, Denner Discount nearby, Brig Simplon-Tourism, SBB Citybistro Brig.

280
There are at least five of us in our tourism project, a number of us based in the office. The dog usually skips around with us on our travels. With small group excursions, Manu can take photographs while she talks about the surroundings, which the participants enjoy, and I can collect short portraits.

281
We are friendly to our guests, as was common in bygone novels. Dear reader, they would write, and we say: Dear guests, we are here for your amusement and to alert your attention. Then we remind them of what we said at the start of the tour, of our conversation about the colours of the rocks, and we ask the group to stand still and look around the Inn Valley, and while they look around it is interesting to watch their faces. At the end of the tour we say that we've milked our time together well, that milking them in the mountains was very pleasant.

282
In the back office, Lucius plays the drums and Sam sings

– music that we play for the tourist group on our phones. Later, Sam calls over the phone: Run, run! Our dog knows his voice and sets off, running up a short slope with his ears pricked, then he hears Stop, stop, that's enough, and then the word back, and he turns around and comes back to the group, hears Stop again, halts and looks happy. We get considerable amounts of tips.

283
Before we say goodbye, we ask the participants what themes they felt were missing, since neither Manu nor I have talked about ski pistes, ski lifts, holiday landscapes or avalanches, barely touched upon the history of Alpine settlements, and have not even mentioned typical local specialities.

284
He's had enough of the tourist idea, Lucius says, and he sings 'It Ain't Necessarily So'.

285
The dog has brown ears, brown eyes, understands around a hundred words, likes open landscapes and has no trouble with intricate altitudes. Bridges are a challenge for him. He has never experienced the narrow old bridle paths or the donkeys tracking along them.

286
In the old days, donkeys frequently plunged to the depths from the bridle paths, the big grey animals falling complete with their freight. Now they graze in occasional front gardens; the old transport methods no longer exist, the donkeys no longer suffer, and there are not many of them left.

287
Manu does not sing. She has no wish to encourage the cliché that black people sing and are musically talented, possess no talents but the musical, and she has no wish to beguile anyone with her life story (life history).

288
Once she told me her parents had died in a car accident after they moved to Switzerland. Another time, she said they had fallen to their deaths in the mountains. The common denominator is that her mother and father died simultaneously, which is not necessarily the case either.

289
Sam says nothing, nothing about the past, even if he's asked; he evades the question and skips to subjects of his choice. All I know is that his and therefore also Manu's father and mother were both musicians, but whether they played in an orchestra or a band or performed as soloists is unclear to me. Manu once mentioned that their mother had taught in Biel, so she may have been a music teacher. Sam voluntarily repeats that he is a mummy's boy and his sister a daddy's girl.

290
Foreign in former times, that too exists. Freely foreign in former times.

291
Lucius had arranged access to a cave or rather a tunnel, where we spent a whole day painting, sketching and writing. Whatever came about would remain unchanged for two

weeks, said the older woman in charge of the place, a smart woman, not elderly, who descended into the tunnel with wellington boots on her feet and pearls around her neck. She showed us the lighting options and said in a pleasantly absent-minded way that it would suit her if we took songs into account in our ideas.

Lucius had found the place so he could steer Manu and me inside a mountain. The other participants came along without a second thought.

292
We were in a deep opening in the mountain, the outer mountain wall was wooded along its lower section, followed further up by a meadow landscape, and we were sitting inside the tunnel. High above our heads untroubled cows grazed on pastures surrounded by rock, yet since they almost never ventured forth onto the brittle stone rock face, they were obviously slightly troubled after all, or at least they respected the stony danger.

Above us the woods, the cows, further up climbers competing on the rocks, and beneath our feet, perhaps, precious and semi-precious stones.

293
Manu and I sat behind one of the two flood lamps in the semi-shadows. Sam came over to us with the others and we drank hot tea together.

294
When Sam was still in London, the six of us once met up

online so he could tell us about the city's music and its offshoots in Switzerland. His camera wasn't working so he was only acoustically present. We listened to our invisible friend's deep voice, saw the five of us on the screen in five squares, our faces slightly distorted – and we will probably not escape these distortions easily. We listened patiently to Sam's ghostly voice. He spoke about blues and soul, baroque music, alphorn and reggae, about Gershwin and other composers. He named singers and bands – had I made notes I could have inserted a long list here – and as he spoke his voice moved further away and came closer again, since he was walking around the room. He paced up and down because he actually wanted to offer us a performance, and he could have broken off because of his camera trouble but he went on speaking. He was talking about listening to music, not seeing it, he said, whereby the seeing had positive side effects but the listening was the main thing. Then he said he was drinking a sip of red wine, and we raised our glasses to him. Thank you, he said. He could see us. Later he spoke of a resonance chamber in the body, of the special role of the diaphragm when a person is singing and also when a person is listening. The diaphragm listens in, he said, though not for the first time; he had mentioned it several times. We nodded, and then he sang. Then he told us about a science programme that talked about a section of the brain where the vocal pitches a person hears are experienced as particularly pleasant or unpleasant, depending on how their own frequencies or antennae are wired, or built. It was all about resonances. Back then, he wanted more precise information or hoped to listen to the programme again, but he had written to the radio station too late and they turned him down. None of us knew anything about neuronal connections with regard to pitches in the brain.

295
We rarely talk of the diaphragm. The German word is remarkable: Zwerchfell. Zwerch is a word for diagonal and Fell once meant skin, though now it means fur, so the Zwerchfell is a diagonal skin, incessantly active, a supporting actor to the lung, a kind of bellows that we ought to be fond of instead of talking constantly about high blood pressure, hearts and prostates.

296
I had once talked about the Christianisation of the Alps and its concurrent music, which Sam disagreed with, although the movies and documentaries dealing with these wild mountains tend to use Central European classical compositions, and it is also interesting that those film series with deliberately related titles such as The Wild Alps, Wild Austria, Wild Switzerland promise a non-domesticated landscape, while the background music is tame and Christian. I shall remain with these thoughts, which Sam laughed about (his head bent back).

297
We had agreed to leave the cave only for lunch, and around noon the woman with the wellingtons summoned us into the fresh air, where she awaited us with barley broth and bacon rolls. After eating, we went back inside the cave and Lucius started tapping on the stone walls again; that was his reference to music. Fortunately, he ventured forth into the deeper realms, so the tapping and knocking was not too

loud. Ruth painted the words *Allegory of the cave* on the wall, in large letters. Manu photographed us all, and while she was switching her two cameras and their lenses, she bent her hands back and forth deep from the wrist. She has the good fortune to be double-jointed.

298
I sat beside the flood lamp and all I noted down was that language begins with the voice; everyone knows it begins with the voice. All speaking is music. I still have the notepad. It smells musty and damp to this day.

299
Not only among mountaineers and climbers are there competitors brave, bold and timid. Cowards and fighters are found elsewhere too.

300
Not only I (and Manu) but the others too felt like foreign bodies in the tunnel. But that's not saying much. Some people thrive on not feeling at home, even enjoy not feeling at home when they're home. Foreignness is an interesting gut feeling.

301
If a person is asked at a party where they come from, it is sometimes a mere question of curiosity. The asker hears a peculiarity in the other person's language and takes the opportunity to find out new things about a more or less faraway place. Ah, Italy, they say, and attempt to continue the conversation in Italian. In another encounter, they might toss in two or three words of Russian.

302
On other occasions, a person is asked where they come from because they seem foreign, and the very question is all about rejection. Aha, the Linzer, Meraner, Tiraner, the Arab, the South American is unmasked. But instead of answering properly, the askee says cheers and raises their glass, and if there are no glasses at hand then they nod. Yes, yes, they say. Then they are tripped up, they fall and they end up in hospital. And still they say nothing about themselves. They may want to cast off what lies behind them, as some animals cast off their skin, their antlers or limbs. In the end they have missing fingers, arms, legs, and then a detective investigates their case.

303
Languages have their own talents, which are associated with certain moods.

In Bündnerland they talk with a different basic mood than in Innsbruck, and it is no help that the Inn sets the tone (of voice) in both places. People from Innsbruck and people from Bündnerland could spend a whole evening rejoicing over the Inn, and still the Bündners would declare afterwards that their language is more honest, while the people from Innsbruck would say their language has more feeling to it. And a woman from Bern who no longer lives in Bern said recently that she was sticking with her soul language.

304
Even though languages keep rolling on and on, they are not avalanches; unlike snow, they do not fall from the sky. They are propelled in the palate, in the stomach area and in the

front and back regions of the brain, certainly also in the mouth, and as soon as a person falls in love with a foreigner, a new tone rolls along with new words, private and intimate words that must be hidden because they sound like betrayal, a betrayal of the so-called soul language, and so the lover or the lovers would do best to move far away, to another country. There, they live together as foreigners, essentially through linguistic expulsion, but at least both of them know the yearning for language and are glad to have fallen in love with throats.

305

A word moves off, bumps into a wall, switches meaning, the bystanders applaud and then the word moves back, switches meaning again (almost generating an alternating current). For example, *meanwhile* moves off and comes back as *mean* and *bad*.

Bad, I'm bad! Bad is suddenly marvellous. Then the word trombone runs into a wall, bounces back, prompts laughter and clapping and returns as a bone.

Now our poor battered word staggers and lurches. It has taken a blow to the left, a blow to the right, unsteady on its feet, but it thinks that hardly any word says exactly what it wants to say.

306

The third rockslide in a matter of days, this time in Wallis. After the rockfall in Raron, the region is blocked off and the inhabitants have to leave their houses.

307
I had a wrong word in my head, couldn't think of the right one; it was buried at first, in the shade.

308
Sam was barely back from London when we met at the osteria. Starved, we launched ourselves upon the scaloppine al limone. Over espresso, Sam took a sheet of paper from his pocket, stood up and said he'd been looking forward for a while to reading aloud to us from this page.

Here comes a game with the letter H. How do you pronounce Theresa? For example, when you think back in anger to Theresa May. Do you pronounce the TH in the middle of the word Penthesilea? When do you say T for a TH spelling and when do you say a clear TH, and why? Do you say L-hasa or Lasa? Where does the H come from? An aspiration from colonial days? But Gandhi, oh Gandhi, he could have stood up to them to tackle the colonialist H. He could have pulled himself together to explain when the European ideas with the ostensibly noble and partly disparaging H-additions began and especially why. Gandhi failed in that single regard, probably because of his affhiliations. Chaste affhiliations. The transcription of pronunciation has an intricate relationship to the ears. H is for those who add lha-di-da. They stick out their pinkies when they drink, they write ph, th, ch and they smile. This aspirational aspirating still exists in p-hotograp-hy, although anyone who can move their thumb or any other finger is capable of taking a foto these days.

309
Later Lucius too spoke standing. The radio news programmes are fans of statistics, he said. As such, they might as well report one day that people are merely hiding behind 70 per cent of words and sentences. The words are bushes, with people squatting behind them.

310
Red-headed Lucius speaks Russian and a good bit of Irish. He is the nephew of the genius who sets off in Altdorf with the most complicated arithmetic problems and offers solutions for his fans shortly afterwards, an emblem of Altdorf, actually crazy, and his athletic nephew is currently trying out non-European idioms to get more of a linguistic overview. Without linguistic overview, we primarily have layers of fog, he says.

311
But there are also times when speakers are intimidated and begin to cower. Language is intimidated and seeks diversions. Sometimes it attempts to say what is important to it in hidden ways, sometimes it hides so as to be spared, and it grows thin, spindly, insignificant.

312
I look for the family tree of languages or words, of all things. I have a linguistic receiver somewhere in my diaphragm (my diagonal skin) for their lineage and their diagonal relationships to other languages (and I am not the only one).

313
The waiter in the osteria, actually La Corona's owner, had

joined us at our table, the dog was asleep, the wolves roamed the mountains and we spoke about various types of roots and about how some believe they have a family tree, believe themselves to be trees that put down roots.

314
Thus, there are the tree people, and there is the soul language.

315
Lost in languages, in all these languages, a whole day spent lost in languages, teetered right in. A day spent on languages, nothing else, verloren in Sprachen, a day-long language odyssey, a language trip.

316
Just in case language is further thinned out and writing becomes obsolete, I am collecting pictograms and can already assemble small stories out of them.

Man / horse / mountain / upwards / tight bends / danger of skidding. Or: Danger of poisoning / open window. Or: Cycle lane / rockslide / snack bar / police.

The pictograms are followed by statistics, usually represented as numbers. Eight-digit, nine-digit, digitised numbers enter the ring. A numbers girl walks along a catwalk and announces them.

Immediately afterwards, the joke sadly plunges to a gruesome death in the valley.

317
Postcard to self: pile, flowery carpet, ocean of colour with isolated striking dabs, primarily yellow, several shades of red. A riot of colour, luminous for an extremely short time before the show is over, but we are left with a few mountain cowslips, even in the crevices (matt green, like Manu's clothing).

318
In the mountains: coming and going, running, climbing, turning, creeping, strolling, roaming, walking, hurrying, sprinting, springing, stalking, wading, wobbling, fleeing, leaving, soaring, bolting, halting, limping, stumbling, teetering, swaying, sliding, falling. Endless possibilities for verbs, and the Alps are nothing if not photogenic.

319
There has been a great blossoming of sculpture schools, skiing schools, climbing schools, hiking schools, and recently also fitness studios and wellness studios. We can only hope for tree schools: Baumschulen, known in English as nurseries. That would conclude my description of the landscape in the mountain regions.

320
At last we were back at the Julier Pass. We watched the car drivers and took photographs. Sam declared he would tidy up the Alps. He would have to remove obvious defects. First of all, he would fill in brittle rock formations and a series of vertical crevices with plaster, glue up smaller rips in the stone and give the far too pointed peaks a more rounded shape. Among other things, he would like to see

how the topographical shoulder drops would look after his reconstruction. The last step would be to paint the plaster surfaces in a pale, calm shade so that the mountains would no longer have to show off the abysmal misfortune that once befell them.

Aside from that, he told us, he had another plan, in which he would switch over a number of massifs. To do so, he would have to saw them off at their feet so as to move them cleanly, and we would play a kind of chess game as we reordered the Alpine landscape. The mountains would be the pieces on the board.

321

The craggy, whitish-yellow Dolomites must not be plastered or moved. What outstanding pillar structures, almost stelae, with corals embedded! Mont Ventoux too must remain untouched. It is the western giant of the Alps.

322

I must not lose sight of the topographical term shoulder drop, and I ought to take heed of watershed too. The English is derived from water plus shed, a calque of our German Wasserscheide, a compound of Wasser (water) plus scheiden (to divide). Our German words for divorce, divide, distinguish, discard, disparate, determined, expire: they all share this scheiden. Wasserscheide contains a clear image for us German speakers. It renders visible how the waterways separate at a (relatively) high point, the streams or rivers move off in distinguishable directions and are divorced from then on, turning away from one another once and for all.

323
Reckenbühlstrasse is still quiet in the best sense. I stand at the window for hours, going out in between, sometimes with the dog; I stand back at the window, sit at one of the two tables, look through my notes, and with my elbow on the tabletop I rest my head on my outstretched fingers, four fingers aligned on my cheekbone, thumb tucked under my chin. As if I were ready for online conversations with image transmission. In my online conversations, I have observed that women look thoughtful with fingers outstretched along their cheeks or their temples and thumbs tucked under their chins. Manu feels compelled to photograph images like these from her screen. Heads resting now on the right hand, now on the left. A performance of attention. At a conference on the subject of the Alps, I counted more than thirty people in one online conversation, all individually observable, and the thoughtful ones were instantly recognisable, especially the women among them. The others were barely noticeable. And one of those displayed in the small squares was making telephone calls on different devices; we saw her speaking, and we saw what she wanted to tell the online conference through her conversations. A new type of preparedness for combat.

324
There are sensational and less noteworthy diseases, so each illness has its own significance. The interesting ones are cancer, Ebola, alcoholism and drugs. Plus accidents in avalanches. Dying of an insignificant illness seems pointless, just as dying is also impersonal if countless people perish in a volcano eruption or an earthquake. Then the eruption or the earthquake are in focus. The situation is

watched more closely if a person is at risk of a significant type of death, because these cases go beyond the illness itself, are a matter of dying and thus of interesting ambiguities.

325
We could speak, on one hand, of a dignified, noble end to a life, and on the other hand of futile, faceless, ahistorical deaths. In any case, the question arises of what to do with the organs.

326
Almost all notes on diseases belong in a separate folder, although accidents also play a role elsewhere. For the time being, though, I want to isolate dying.

327
I shall start a folder to contain the topics not otherwise mentioned. These are still under construction. I now have a list of Sam's subjects, which both of us avoid. He has sent me seventeen lines of brief explanation of each term. After both taking note, we shall redact the lines, paint them black, for these terms are generally passed-around, oft-repeated matters.

328
In the days when I was still firmly intending to keep separate diaries, I planned a series of age descriptions within the portraits section. There are many ways in which to age, differing age personalities, possibilities for maturing and deteriorating. I wanted to call the subject of my first portrait A, the second B, and then continue alphabetically.

329
Older people are being introduced to the world of the internet; young friends, neighbours and grandchildren help them along. That is why old people are not visible in the streetscape. They are sitting in front of their screens.

330
On a number of mornings, I have seen a man of around eighty in a copse near Reckenbühlstrasse, an alert old man with white hair. He seems tense in profile. He strides slowly through the woods almost every morning, and once, when I was sitting on a bench, he sat down next to me. Neither he nor I intended to make conversation; we were united on that from the outset. He looked around, and I looked at his shoes, soft as butter.

331
Theoretically, the sketches I originally called flimericks belong with the portraits.

There once was a man who did not believe in the duplication of stories but was curious by nature, who one day walked up to himself in Steinbach and was so amazed that he bumped into himself, and that broke the story in two.

In Steinberg lives an exemplary man with a neatly combed ponytail, who looks early modern, thinks hard and is enterprising.

I know a woman in Steinach who thinks hard about herself and enjoys presenting herself as a thinker. She writes about books that she does not read.

A woman writes from Steinau that she is not faring well. Yesterday, though, she tripped another woman up, and that woman, she writes, is now simply gone.

From Steinwald, the centre of the community, the news came last week that K. M. had got fat and would no longer be a danger to anyone. Wishful thinking.

All the things we see in people! It's enough to make a person go blind.

332

AI does everything for me. I am AI and my name is Aileen, she says. She was trained at creative writing schools, and she says openly that my way of writing is not her thing. She will begin by processing my pieces on a biographical basis and embellishing them. I am welcome to go on writing for myself, she says. She will not delete my work – so I know its deletion is pre-programmed.

I could have sworn this had really happened to me, by Skype or something, but it was probably a bad dream; I have been having a lot of bad dreams lately.

333

Later, we went into the larger room, where we were to sing. We bandits; bandits, they called us. People from various countries sat alongside us. Manu and I would never have thought of ourselves as foreigners, but they said: sit down, stay calm. A man from Turkey, born in Berlin, danced almost naked for ten minutes or so, which caused much agitation and we thought to run away in all the upheaval, but security men stopped us at the door and waved us back with friendly gestures.

334
Crashing in the middle of a text. Pause for breath, lost threads.

335
Though Sam throws away his sketches, notes and even personal letters and only files away the drafts he needs for the office, he has twice tried to persuade me to start a walk-in archive, and now he has even presented me with sketches. One for nine different-sized rooms, one for fifteen. Everything should be fully walkable for both presentation and imagination, he said. We walk people through individual ideas, we walk our way through your ideas, we walk and walk, he said, and he wanted me to count up the topics of my planned notebooks so as to house them in his rooms. Weeks ago, we talked once again about daily notes kept in parallel, about daily foods, daily phone calls, about portraits, dreams and quotes, and I mentioned the gigantic man from Hamburg in Venice, the prototype for multiple bookkeeping. Sam cannot break free from that story and neither can I, but Sam seems to want to match up to that man, another architect, which is why he sketched the walk-in diary.

In his model, a clown would guide the visitors through the archive rooms, addressing them here and there, and would continually enrich the exhibition with new details, because new material would by nature keep coming. The ideas on the individual topics go on, on and on. Even on the subject of mountains alone! Who could present them plausibly until their expiration date, which is one day certain to come! In the archive rooms, there would be pictures and acoustic recordings of pieces, plus the clown's commentaries. This clown would barely ever laugh; he would be, or rather he is, an experienced exhibition accompanier.

He recently spent a month travelling with donkeys, which ought to appeal to me, Sam said, and when I nodded he asked me again for the topics so as to place them in each room. Hey presto, he said, hey presto, and he went on undeterred despite me shaking my head. So the clown walks the visitors through the rooms, talking briefly about the pieces, which anyone can read on the corkboards or listen to on tape. The curly-haired man walks ahead and can turn off in either direction, just like thoughts can, and it is best to see these turn-offs spatially, Sam says. Sometimes the clown sits down in a corner and lets visitors wander through the rooms on their own.

He would not necessarily cry if I didn't agree, he said, because he never cries otherwise. Then he showed me how the clown could even tell stories as a circus act. One of the rooms was about falling from the Matterhorn, Sam said, and therefore a picture appears of the Matterhorn with a falling man, tumbling downwards. The clown points a long stick at the photo or the painting and tells stories from the fallen man's life. At the second picture, he points the stick at the mourners. The third picture shows a black-clad widow.

Where does Sam get his stories from? He said that in one

room, the clown would even show a film about the construction of the Gotthard railway tunnel, which might go well with my ideas about mountains, and he paced back and forth in his gangling walk to convince me. He finished off by saying he had also designed a number of rooms for Manu's photography, but she had looked at him just as incredulously as I.

336
After her photo book came out, Manu said she would concentrate on children's faces; she did not have enough. She too had problems capturing them, it was not just the painters, especially the old painters who tended to present children as geriatrics, as plasticine models. She also had to investigate the laughter that sets in after a major shock, she said, the laughter after a helpless shock.

337
It was midday; no church bells nearby. The former dinosaurs, now birds, cooed, chirped, croaked, trilled through the air. We were sitting on a stone bench and Milly was with us; we sat long and hard on a cold stone bench near a reservoir. What is really erotic? Milly asked. The question of what is erotic does not go unasked in the Alps, only the question is too serious, too loaded with meaning.

338
What does happiness look like? Milly asked a little later.

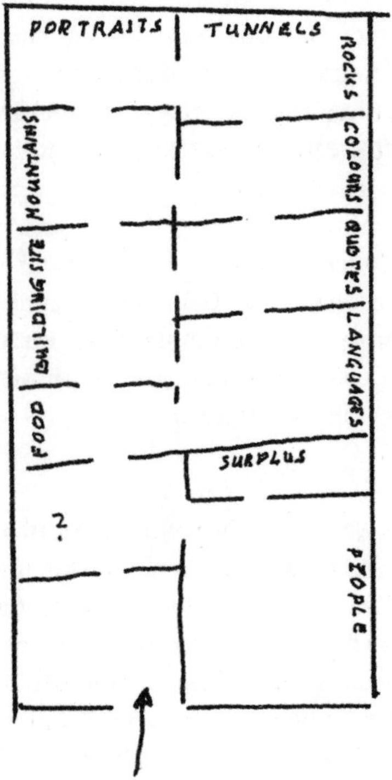

PORTRAITS
TUNNELS
ROCKS
MOUNTAINS
COLOURS
BUILDING SITE
QUOTES
LANGUAGES
FOOD
SURPLUS
2.
PEOPLE

339
Scree, mountainsides, public transport and the colours of sunsets shall be mixed in with portraits and earlier encounters, shuffled over and over as if the topics were playing cards, dealt face-down. Then everyone turns over their own cards and tries to work with the details they've been dealt. Everyone holds different notes in their hand, each around ten, and the rest of the cards remain in the stack. After the game they are shuffled anew, dealt anew, and again the players see splinters of stories that they order and latch together so as to create a passable ten-card story.

340
Suddenly, the police pop up beside the card table, two officers sneering down at us. Gambling is banned, we must know that, they say, handcuffs at the ready. But we pretend we are acting in a movie and stare passively into the distance, as if we had not understood a word.

341
I like the extras who play police officers in crime shows, who set off packed tightly together in full kit, their knees slightly bent. They stick with their knee positions even at a trot. Perhaps it looks the same on real police business, and maybe they use police officers for these film scenes to give them an easy side job on the set. They have their original equipment and know how to behave without instruction. They're on police business. It starts with an emergency in the mountains, at the Lötschen Pass. Eight smugglers, as they were once called, have just been caught, eight experienced mountain workers. Their mobile phone data is evaluated, but first they must get into police cars.

The officers hold one hand above each of their heads so they don't get hurt getting in, and also to show who's in charge. This ambiguous gesture says a great deal.

342
There's something we have overlooked.

343
We were at the Julier Pass on a cloudless, windless day with long views, and Sam wanted to take advantage of the good weather to glue up the unappealing rifts in the rock, plaster them over and paint the freshly patched places. Lucius preferred a coat of lacquer, perhaps in the same shade of red as his hair.

344
On the rock faces, grey-green and matt green mountain cowslips protrude between stones, and in the green spaces on the Furka Pass, isolated violet and purple flowers blossom, just briefly. The violet evening sky disappears in a matter of minutes. Vivid pale brown, half-dark sand brown beside black. Matt grey beside dark blue: not the sapphires in the rock; I mean the Lac Bleu.

Green beside blue, landscape painting. White limestone rock beside billowing green. Bleached yellow reminiscent of bruised white. Dusky pink, almost salmon-coloured, beside it bright orange, as if the salmon were poisoned.

I recall pictures from the 1960s with towels, sweaters, scarves and bedlinen in a particular shade of orange. That cheap dye had nothing in common with fruity oranges, though it was supposed to remind us of fruits; nor with the royal House of Orange, nor with landscapes, and nothing at all in common with mountains. It was a chemical dye mix, probably with its own identifying number, agreed in advance with designers. But the moment orange or rust-red remind me of cave paintings, the colours recover.

345
Recently, a school for colours and their perception opened in Brunnen. Handouts were handed out for the occasion. For example: 'What is Iris like? Is she heavenly, earthly, never morose? / Iris is blue. / Does everyone think of an i for blue? / Is iris the flower blue, or is Iris the woman blue?'

346
Inherited words: the name Lienz occurs frequently in the Alps. Lienz is usually a place name. And then there is Linz. Lech is another strange migratory word. Lago and lake belong with Lech, but not lechzen: gasping. Perhaps Lech originally meant water. The Lauche is a minor river in the Swiss Central Plateau. The Lauche was once rich in trout and pike.

347
Languages are repeatedly destabilised; ways of speaking waver in the Alps, but not only in mountain landscapes. Here the words fall and smash apart, in other places they dry out, silt up, or they haunt us as ghosts. (Blessèd is one such word.) Then again, some words stick firm. They are immune to all attacks.

348
Mountains are not the most difficult topic. They unarguably exist, visibly, are a product of the disquiet inside the earth, poor witnesses to the shifting of several tectonic plates, a severe accident from the rocks' point of view since they were tipped, broken, divided multiple times and shifted, and after being shifted they were lifted and broken again; in time lapse, we would hear grinding and groaning.

What is that groaning! The mountains are calling you. Even the very youngest know the song, as I recently learned. 'The Mountains are Calling' is an eternal song, an evergreen as they say, although the poor mountains are only green up to their middles, at best; but they call, and even the skiers have at the back of their mind that they are connected with the innards of the mountains. If they were not connected with their innards, they would not keep speeding down their steep snowy slopes.

The restacked, piled-high, high-blown rocks stare day and night at the sky.

A bigger problem is the question of wit, wit in general and where the Alps and wit are connected. In the end, the Alps themselves are a joke, the poor things.

349
The idea of the chess match in the Alps appeals to me, simply because of the overview, because of the long view of the entire mountain landscape. However, it would be better to talk of a board game, where the rules are easier, in which the mountains switch places. National borders

do not get in the way; the swap counts regardless. The separate mountains and massifs are the pieces on the board; in German board games, we call them stones.

350
Just seen the Dolomites. I rarely associate the Alps with beauty, but in this case I felt instantly drawn. I would not like to climb their tower-like formations, but I would like a good place to observe them at length. What outstanding, upstanding pillar structures, almost stelae, and with coral in the rock.

351
The Dolomites, Mont Ventoux, the Julier Pass and the Schafkopf! Once I sat with a local acquaintance in Kastanienbaum on Lake Lucerne, opposite us a clear view of Mount Rigi, and my acquaintance said the Rigi had dolled itself up for us. That was the first time I'd heard that expression, in the small town of Kastanienbaum. A clearly visible mountain has put on a good face. Visibility is the be all and end all in the Alps, and the fact that the mountains themselves play an active role by making themselves look good, for insiders, is impressive, which is why I keep this Rigi episode in the back of my mind, though my favourites are the aforementioned four. But even between these four I could not move constantly to and fro, have an apartment here, a house there and along the way visit amiable hosts like Gabriel Epp in Uri, while others cannot ever move away from their original places and do not want to resettle even from the north side of a mountain to its south.

352
And what is resettling! Is it a constantly repeated settling, an iterative verb?

353
The waggish Herr Epp said recently that he had no carpets in his rooms so as to banish verrucae, toenail fungus and all kinds of bugs. Verrucae, he said, are repeatedly brought in, and he wants nothing to do with them. Herr Epp has given great thought to equipping his mountain house.

354
The area west of Mont Ventoux could be described as lowland, so gigantic is the difference between the mountain and the lower zone adjoining it to the west. The Alps end with the extended Mont Ventoux, the mountain clearly peripheral; more than that, strictly speaking it is not part of the Alps, but we would have to dig deep, geologically, for an explanation, and no one could imagine a more successful west end, anyway. West end! A term that deserves to become established. The Giant of Provence is thirty-five kilometres long, rounded on its southern side and otherwise craggy, descending almost vertically. I looked it up in my atlases, and what I know mainly is pictures of the region sent by an acquaintance of Ruth's, a woman from Munich whom I call an informant or a coach, and I have learned from her that up on the chine in good weather, you can see all the way to the Mediterranean, deep into the Alps and even to the edge of the Pyrenees. She also described the everwhite peak, the massif's endlessly long, naked white limestone slope. Ventoso, she calls the mountain, and she has experienced how windy it is up there

first-hand on a hike. Once a year, at least once a year, she goes there, to Grignan, fifty kilometres as the crow flies from the giant, and she sees it from there as if she could reach out and touch. On the one hand there's the view of the distance from the mountain, on the other hand the view of the resting giant from the distance, she wrote in an email, once again with photographic accompaniment.

355
Once, my coach told me of a Madame Da Prato near Avignon who makes the best crespéou, omelettes slathered layer by layer with various vegetables, so well described that I think I know this Madame Da Prato and her crespéou too. This popular layered dish is a topographical signpost, pointing along a path of layered dishes all the way down to the Mediterranean, then on to Italy, the southern Slavic countries, to Greece and to Turkey.

356
The standalone Mont Ventoux, the Dolomites and the Schafkopf must remain untouched in our board game with the mountains.

The game is about focusing our view of the mountains. We can see how the mountains and massifs are swapped over, the Matterhorn for the Großglockner, the Karwendel range for the Glarus Alps. The candidates are sawn off neatly low down at their feet, expelled, excavated, excoriated and carefully rearranged. They may not be broken. New satellite images come about on the basis of the rearrangements, and new branches of research come about on the basis of the new images.

357
On the Schafkopf and its nearby lakes, I wanted to look for the former summer vacationists. There once was a time of summer vacationists. Writers female and male would sit down together, Schnitzler, Hofmannsthal and Thomas Bernhard. They did not arrive together but they did come to be together, and when I booked my trip to the sheep-headed mountain, I thought the six of us could stage a fitting quotation rotation. If we sat together by a lake we could quote the former summer vacationists, and the idea of a conversation together in the sun still appeals to me despite having cancelled the trip, though I had planned to make it alone.

358
The Schafkopf and the socialising by the lake at Altaussee. Those mountain lakes where illustrious visitors met up, including individuals who still interest me now and whose presence we book as historical, as if they had considered themselves historical in their own present day, as if they were quotations of themselves.

359
Each Alpine lake has its personal moods, its viewing conditions, lighting conditions, its very own surroundings on its shores; they are easy to distinguish, which is true of all lakes, but I shall stick with the Alps.

360
The one I know best is Lake Zug. I spent a year watching the water in changing weather, changing light. The lake is a special place for me, but to compare this well-known

landmark to a lodestar would be too weighty, and a weight would quickly sink to the bottom of the lake, and so on.

361
Milly, Sam's ex, became a third mate on Lake Geneva after they separated, and Lake Geneva is incomparable for her. She and Sam were both twenty-two when they divorced, she says, and she adds details the others have never mentioned; but I do not want to know such new things. Lake Geneva remains her property, Lake Uri belongs to Lucius, and Ruth has the port in Lucerne.

362
Anyone can butt in and claim that the name for the Alps stems from Arabic, since words beginning with Al come from Arabic. Al Pine. The real origin of the word is interesting. Alp or Alm. Originally a mountain pasture, a Celtic or even older word for every single mountain pasture.

363
Ruth suggests setting up collection boxes in various places for linguistic scholars, for donations to support etymologists and their explanations, so they don't run out of steam because their departments garner too little attention and are granted only meagre funding. We request collection boxes worldwide for etymologists, so as to know which word clambered out of where. Lucius has already paid in.

364
Were the weight of each massif to be measured – the pressure they exert on the deepest layers of the tectonic plates – the results would be confusing. The pressure of the stone

masses is gigantic, and were it to be reduced, the tectonic plates would no doubt rise correspondingly.

365
The only disturbing thing, basically, is that the mountains, especially the celebrities among them, are seen as eternal creations, as if they were, firstly, indestructible and, secondly, a ladder up to heaven, neither of which is true.

366
Landscape painting. A view of the mountains' bodies, of the rocks and the glaciers.

367
Often, several similar mountain shapes are positioned alongside one another, almost like copies. The mountains are similarly sharp, their flanks have almost identical inclinations, the layers of rock, visible as lines, run in the same direction. These neighbours suffer comparable fates, the same geological blows have befallen them.

368
Postcard to self: Individual mountains cannot be declined, neither forward nor back. Their flanks can be shaved off, their peaks hewn into shape, they weather of their own accord and we can even burrow through the mountains' bellies, but no one can bend, decline or conjugate the mountains.

369
The mountain ranges running west or east are a flip-book for Sam, the Alpine Divide the guideline for the

somersaulting pictures. The series of mountains along the north–south axis also produces a flickering film.

370
My neurologist tells me not to torture myself if I can only remember isolated names of mountains. Even if I were interested in all their names it would be too much of a challenge, and the names surely don't interest me much, he says.

371
She is having a creative crisis, says Manu. She can neither snap the children's faces floating past her in flagrante, nor capture the strange smiles of the injured, those who almost died or cannot yet grasp the danger they have been in. She keeps harking back to one particular face, a man whose house had burned down, and just afterwards he said with a laugh that he was left with nothing but the clothes he was wearing. She had experienced such a laugh amid shock only once before, she said, and now she was seeking such a face in vain. Aside from which, she is short of laughers who don't constantly show their teeth. Laughter these days is a matter of dentistry, displaying the health of our teeth, highly beneficial for an entire industry. She herself could show off a fairly white set of teeth but that is out of the question, she says; it is nothing to do with friendliness, she says, not at all. Incidentally, one should never bare one's teeth to cats, otherwise they leap away or extend their claws. On encountering cats, it is better to give them a tired blink.

372
Postcard: A constant baring of repaired and prepared teeth,

teeth in faces of all kinds. And the ancient Egyptians consumed fruit in the morning for dental hygiene.

373
Archaeologists have always been glad to find skulls with full sets of teeth or as many teeth as possible, to help determine the deceased's age, nutritional status or diseases, and perhaps linguistic scholars now know how to determine the language of the dead based on the positions of their teeth. Learning new things about the dead and their teeth requires several types of scholar, with each of their areas of expertise. Scientists are surely not distracted by the fact that bare skulls seem to grin. They concentrate instead on the exposed jaw, concentrate according to their own set of questions. The division of labour has been more or less worked out over time, but their future colleagues will be more likely faced with dental implants and will have to change their methods. The geologists, meanwhile, stick to the limestone deposits in the northern and southern Alps and never think about teeth, only shells and fishbones.

374
The languages in the Alps, their histories. The ancient, old and new people of the mountainscape. The even older, eternally alive viruses and bacteria nestled deep in the rock and underneath the glaciers. A place as ancient as its rock.

375
Sam spent two days out with his recorder on matters Swiss German, and said that people can distinguish the slightest sounds, pricking up their ears and hearing precisely who comes from where, down to a few kilometres. And why not.

It happens that way in most places, not just in the mountains. What they barely take note of is pitch. People don't notice squished head tones or nervously leaping singsong. But the German between Heidelberg and Berlin, between Hannover and Munich, sounds similarly foreign to their ears.

Sam's research took place at four locations. Lucius went with him because Sam feared hostility to his dark skin in the mountains, despite his Swiss dialect. Together, the two of them got the job done.

376
Six-way conversations are perfectly possible, temporarily even with more people, for instance with Gabriel Epp, with whom even twelve people could stay silent; and by the way he needs a der in front of his name in German, der Gabriel like the Swiss say, not just Gabriel, otherwise he would be wrested out of his familiar surroundings.

377
Shortly after the storm, I came down from the mountain house to Altdorf; after my mountain isolation I expected a lively place, but instead the empty streets and lack of passers-by were the real sensation, and ever since then I've seen all the people sitting in front of their screens; in all their homes they sit in front of screens, I look up at the facades of apartment buildings and see the illuminated windows, venture a glance into houses and there too they sit in front of their monitors, but Sam is allergic to the term digital (and digital age). It is probably on his list of rejected words. The last time I said it he put his hands over his ears.

378
Autumn in the Alps, as early as August. Several shops are vacant in all the villages (self-echo, I have mentioned it before). Sam calls Manu's photo space, a former newsagent, a clink, a jail in other words, but transforming a paper shop into a workplace for photos is not a bad solution. From her clink, she can photograph the development of the other shops. There will be autumn shots, an Alpine autumn in mid-August, pensive and foggy, appealing; it will take some getting used to.

379
In this favourable weather, an American arrives in Zürich by private jet, flanked by two bodyguards. A civilised entrance. This landing is followed by a drive to Bündnerland.

380
In a crossword puzzle I came across the word vassals; these would be the bodyguards, essentially. The American, a New Yorker, lands with his protectors to consult an architect in Bündnerland. They consult about extending an existing chalet and plans for a new, larger building. The bodyguards carry guns, the New Yorker (with the architect) will take possession of an area in the Alps, and the architect will complete a work of art with the project. This description is complicated because it is about a New Yorker, about his property in the Alps, and at the same time about the architect's artwork, about vassals who might possibly shoot, and that does not yet even cover all aspects; to what extent are the resulting buildings an artwork, and is a property in the Alps an asset on paper: a stock or a share? What happens to the owner of the Alps, and is the New Yorker with

his guards and his architect simply a rock-getter tied up in an internet game?

381
I am honest with the Alps, I have never claimed to have conquered a peak, I have never climbed the Gotthard or the Matterhorn. The Matterhorn is an absurdity, talked up for tourists. At night the horn stares up at the sky, and yet I have begun to develop feelings for the monstrosity. Through my preoccupation, I have come to know the horn a little, and that knowing is not unimportant. Uh-oh, says Sam.

382
Lucius has an excellent head for figures, rather like his mad uncle in Altdorf, but he doesn't do sums for people; he is attracted to other numbers. The earth is around four point four billion years old, he tells us; the youngest mountains are only a few hundred million in, and many of the flattened, worn-away mountain landscapes, usually called uplands, are several times older, lower and older. The tabletop mountains in Guyana, rarely mentioned South American highlands, he says, are an incredible one point seven billion years old. How am I to imagine that, dear Lucius? No answer. Years ago, he went with a friend, saw the ancient territory of high plateaus, level, bony mountain surfaces, and he and the friend feasted on hot tortillas in the region, tried out a wide range of different tortillas.

383
Murderlust first came about approximately in the Cambrian period, as revenge against those who have done us ill,

and also out of pure desire for destroying another person, which is in vogue these days, Lucius says, and he tells us that a man bit through his own wife's throat on the linguistic border in Steinbach. And Sam says the inventor of unruly crime stories was Edgar Allan Poe, an artful inventor who could have told such tales. Wrong, says Lucius. The inventors were the Greeks, the Greeks at the very latest.

384
The current issues raise the question as to whether holiday travel is a human right. Are holidays a question of human rights? There are rising and ebbing issues, and their swaying makes some people seasick.

385
If no questions, then no answers.

386
Not travelling is brave, Manu says, and Ruth hugs her. Bravery is not travelling, travelling is not brave, not every trip is brave, says Manu.

387
If at all, she would tour the mountainscape of Castile, says Manu. Each to their own, she says. She would like to spend days flying over that landscape, at some point.

388
Postcard to self: I have lost a number of sentences, left them behind somewhere, and now I miss them.

389
The Carpathians are structured into various sections, horizontal or vertical division being most common.

390
First, though, the Pyrenees, so I don't have to turn around later and move westwards (conserving energy), and before that I ought to mention the Ardennes in the northwest. Travelling through them, I saw them as Shakespearean stage mountains. A good landscape for quotes.

391
I conquered the western Pyrenees from the passenger's seat, the abyss to my right, two small children perched behind me. We drove on and on, always along the outer edge of the rock face, and I thought my stomach would be ripped out of my body, not my heart; in such cases we speak of the heart, but I thought my stomach would be ripped out. After this audacious drive, we ended up on the southern side of the mountain range in a Spanish bodega, and there the owner said she loved driving across the pass in the dark and the rain.

392
In the bodega, a man came up to us and said we absolutely had to take a trip to Santiago de Compostela. Later, it turned out that he had not been to Santiago himself, the city of his dreams, but he wanted to send us there; he wanted to get there once, at least with his advice.

393
Years later, I read Julio Llamazares's oppressive description

of the Pyrenees. Through his novel *The Yellow Rain*, sadly little known here, I have an idea of the mountain structures, the former mountain villages in the rugged area and their sad depopulation. A contemporary parallel to the earlier depopulation in the high Alpine regions.

394
What I would most like to do is stare out of a warm thermal lake, earnest and attentive like a grey or brown macaque.

395
Landscape description: ultramarine.

396
Landscape description: Lavender, Mediterranean, a view of the distant Dinaric mountains from an island in the Adriatic. The calming lavender islands have sneaked into advertising, lavender to help us sleep. In the old days, so Ruth says, the floral-scented islands were a travel destination.

397
One contrast to the Alps is the flat desert, which can only be survived well cocooned. Veiled up in the sandy desert, in the Namib, bundled up in the high Alps, swathed in furs in the Siberian Plateau, brightly coloured scarves over faces in the Andes.

398
Am I talking about something experienced or something I am imagining? The horses in the Namibian desertscape, the audacious stallions and mares, have learnt to go without water for long periods, and I know them from films,

that's for sure. These animals, left behind more than a hundred years ago, give birth to foals, even rear some of their foals to adulthood, but all in all their numbers are falling; the horses are wasting away, dying of thirst.

399
Mighty island mountains rise majestically from the flat terrain. This is a quote from a film. The majestic in this case is the sharp, needle-like granite elevations in the middle of the southwest African desert.

400
Lowland in sight, plains, expansive views. The expansive landscape in Hamburg, Berlin, London and also in Paris. Endless expanses. A man sauntering London's level landscape is a city flâneur; in non-urban plains he might be a drifter. A flâneur is a city person, not necessarily a poor hobo. He enjoys the view of the city and his unhindered progress, and he enjoys knowing the city's streets and districts. He sits down in a pub now and then, walks on after that. His name is Flavio. A wanderer in the mountain world is rarely a flâneur.

401
In the starkly curved Carpathians I know only the inner arc, and only certain points of that area. The mountain formations in this inner arc are not particularly high, but they squat together impenetrably dense and dark green.

402
For the first time (a remarkable turn of events!) I stayed in a hunting hotel, in a symmetrically designed, once

well-maintained building. One wing on the left, an identical wing on the right, constructed in the late nineteenth or early twentieth century. The left wing housed the dining room, with deer antlers and bear skulls on the left and right walls, beside several framed mirrors. Stairs, fitted with threadbare carpets, led on the left and right to the first floor, and in my room a yet older patterned layer peeped out from behind old, half-torn-off wallpaper. I got into bed in my buttoned-up raincoat and eavesdropped on tipsy conversations from the dining room. In the morning, however, the stairwell smelled of freshly brewed coffee as if everything were suddenly alright. But then the waiter brought a tray to my breakfast table with hot water, Nescafé and tea bags. As he walked towards me he held the tray high above his head, a real skill.

403
Another time, a good hundred kilometres further east, I had a room with three beds. What riches, I thought, and since I was to stay there for three nights I wanted to spend each night in a different bed. As I began to unpack, a woman approached me with open arms: my interpreter, who slept the next three nights in the middle bed, me by the window; while the third bed was occupied by a bleach-blonde Croatian woman with whom we had a language barrier.

404
Postcard: The room's windows are open. From the road I hear semi-deep, diluted male voices, as if on the run from their own sound. An eavesdropping affair.

405
Northeast of Cluj (in the western Inner Carpathian arc) there was a rest stop with a bar for lorry drivers. When we arrived in the early evening they had only a single room for the two of us, but it was not yet ready; we were told to come back later. We waited at a nearby café, where we were served nice pale bread. Though such delicacies are famous all over central Eastern Europe, we could only dream of exquisite open sandwiches topped with ham, sliced egg, salmon, gherkins and aspic. Hours later, we returned to the rest stop and the strongly made-up woman behind the reception desk, or behind the bar, handed us the key and the bedlinen without a word. We were to make the bed ourselves. The sheets were still damp. When we tried to object, the lorry drivers turned their backs on us. We settled the bill and slept in the car.

406
Postcard to self: We ended up in a hotel room with a blood-stained mattress. Probably an unexpected childbirth at this crime scene, a woman raped, or two women on their periods. Bloody life.

407
The hotels, boarding houses, room-renters and hostels have us guests as their prey, us with our alternating feelings when we surrender ourselves, sleeping, in unaccustomed rooms. In the morning, a stranger's false teeth in the shared bathroom, though the memory was to be of one last night together. That night might show itself from its positive side again as soon as the false teeth are forgotten, though that is unlikely. Events like to join up, latch on to each other as if

you had spent the night with a stranger's teeth, and such amalgamations would be well suited to a hotel diary. Episodes in hotels with and without missteps.

408

(Loosely based on Chekhov.) He knelt before her. She knelt before him, he knelt before her, she before him, he knelt, she knelt. A sketch based on a lasting image, but at least it's an image, a truth. And then he knelt again before her, later she before him, and since one could speak of passions, things proceeded similarly the next day and even a week later too.

409

What is inclination! He rocks his baby. A grandfather is standing outside the hotel, white-haired, in sandals without socks, rocking a baby in his arms, shaking it in a friendly manner. The two of them are a family, one person divided in two. The grandfather, with a scarf as a head-covering, holds himself in his arms, and from a room on the third floor watches a man who has spent all night listening to 'Rock Me Baby'.

410

He gradually sawed up the bed, having snuck the electric tool with a sound muffler into the room the day before; the slats quietly fell apart bit by bit in the night. There was no wardrobe in the room, only built-in shelves and clothes rails, which he also sawed up, and he chopped up the table as well. He left the chairs as they were; they were plastic. He carried all the separate parts quietly out of the building down to the riverbank and threw them in. He apologised at reception the next morning for the previous night's disturbance but the woman gestured that he had been no trouble. Once he left the hotel, he was never seen again.

411
The Carpathians with their starkly curved crest are an icon, bilious green, bear brown and wolf grey. Unlike the Alps, well matched in age, they are shocking more for their extensive, impenetrable green than for bare, craggy rockscapes.

412
I have never encountered vicious mythical beasts and their unending malevolence, and I would like to repeat this sentence several times over. All the things that are said! How would those vicious mythical creatures get to the Carpathians!

413
Docile brown bears and docile wolves are in competition and usually have space enough to avoid one another; they are not the problem.

414
From a Central European point of view, the mountain peaks are pushed eastwards. For a simplified overview, they are outsourced eastwards with all their interior stories, and during this shifting of the mountains, the interior stories are not the only thing spilled in the caves.

415
At least the Carpathians are prepared.

416
Dark brown bears roam the mountains with their remarkable intelligence; but then again, they once had to serve as dancing bears, and not just once, dancing on leashes and with rings through their noses for laughing audiences, which is understandable in that bears' movements are adorable, they look heartfelt,

417
and the question: who looks adorable and who is forced to join in against their will? is remarkable and falls silently off a cliff

418
and also the dark, free-roaming bears in the mountains have particularly adorable movements even without an audience to dance for. How they place each leg, their paws! They were originally related to wolves, and yet they cannot mate with them; it doesn't work, though wolves can procreate with all existing kinds of dogs. Yet astoundingly, the bear species is visibly prominent in many dog breeds.

419
After the fall, those present were shocked and initially silent; they couldn't speak, could neither think nor speak. Only after a long period of paralysis did they speak of the incident, and even then, they spoke as if other people had experienced a shock, not them, the poor switched-over people,

420
after a fall all thoughts are switched off, the fallen horses are dead (hunting was once common practice; the flight

animals fled, fell over a cliff and lay dead at its foot, and it was a kind of Western; not a crime show, a Western. How often I have thought this!).

421
If bears are cornered and caught they are converted once and for all, their heads are switched off and then they dance. Wolves, however, leap swiftly away, or else they get shot. (Wolf diary, including dogs.)

422
I am probably most interested in how someone reacts to an unexpected and dangerous blow. How they fall silent. Some smile, beside themselves like after a fall, after sudden pain. The speed at which a body falls is also interesting.

423
Is there something we have overlooked?

424
Sometimes there are five of us, sometimes seven, and there is a second group opposed to us (comparable to the Montagues and Capulets). Our opposing group flies all around the world, which we should also love to do, were we not wiser and more considerate than them. We know it's better to stay calm, and we have ourselves under control. They, though, are endlessly travelling, always in motion, and one of them is currently having two spectacular chalets built in a respected Central European mountainscape. The architects are his shares, the new buildings and the Alps are his stocks. At this very moment, the entire band of opponents is visiting this man. They stand opposite us but they overlook us. These

people are surrounded by their bodyguards. (We might bring in Prokofiev's *Romeo and Juliet* in John Neumeister's choreography at this point, the Stuttgart staging: the enemies leaping at each other with legs long, almost flying, hunting, which looks haunting.) Perhaps there is a third group, aiders and abetters, not key at the moment; they are part and parcel with the bodyguards, a complex story, and the travel-obsessed enjoy complexity, opacity, they like complications, while we seek solutions to crime stories.

425
A good ten years ago, the rarely travelling Manu met a man from the opposing group. She said she was Juliet, and since he was her Romeo his travel-obsessed people mocked him as an ignoramus. For a while, ignoramus and Romeo were identical terms, and then the man disappeared off the face of the earth, simply vanished, Manu said. And since I now know of the wealth of caves in the Carpathians, many of which are under public protection, I can imagine her Romeo in one of those grottoes. This is something Manu does not like to imagine, with her disinclination towards caves, and I don't wish to plumb that dislike. I have long since agreed with her that not everything must be plumbed. I nodded at her, and she snapped a shot as I did so, not exactly flattering. Later, she said that Romeo had never existed; I shouldn't take everything literally.

426
In one of the Carpathian caves, researchers found a 48,000-year-old bone flute; in other caves, fire pits and ancient penis bones, which can only come from animals (bears, wolves, etc.), not from humans.

427
Caves are easy to represent in pictograms; extinguished fire pits are more difficult. If the flame symbol, which stands for fire or danger of fire, is crossed out diagonally, it could also mean fire is prohibited. Perhaps the symbols of flames should be turned upside down as if blazing towards the ground, to indicate that the fire is in the past. Yet past fire is not really important these days; there are more than enough current fires, including across immense stretches, wildfires of sheer unimaginable proportions. These major fires are logged as statistics; these statistics follow the pictograms and are usually represented as numbers.

428
A man stands in his bathroom listening to the latest statistics on the news, numbers of different sizes which he cannot remember. Our nerves are on edge at the moment, he says to himself.

429
Chattering, chinwagging, gassing, gabbling, prattling, tattling, blabbering, in shafts and in shifts.

430
I could describe the man in the bathroom battling with his memory in more detail, so as not to lose sight of my portraits, I thought, while Manu told us about her time in Madrid and showed us, Ruth and me, a photo of her teacher named Paco. This Paco was an admirer of Vilém Flusser, she said, meaning she was now speaking simultaneously of two photography fans, of Paco and of Prague's Vilém Flusser, whom the Madrileño had apparently quoted

multiple times with the statement that a picture representing a landscape simultaneously places itself in front of the landscape. That applied to her own portraits as well, she said, and Flusser's words must be repeated often, she added, since they also applied to written portraits and landscapes. A picture that represents a landscape places itself in front of the landscape.

431

Where were we? Wit fell off a cliff, is lying face-down in the valley. In the obscene valley bottom, Lucius would say, and after the fall comes the great silence.

432

Dead calm, astounding calm. All the streets are empty, but only for a while and then thousands pass by at once, packed in side by side, striding closely together, except the streets are empty again after that, deathly silence sets in, no one to be seen, then later small groups pass by and soon there are several thousand people, packed so tight they can barely make headway; they are photographed and filmed by several drones. A short time later the streets are abandoned again, deserted, and it takes a while for the wave of thousands to roll up again and inch its way forward.

433

Ruth organised a pie evening in Reckenbühlstrasse. She stood at the end of the table and said that the residents, the hosts in other words, had just called to say they couldn't come, despite having promised. Another time, was their message. So the pie convention was for six, there were six of us. That is a maths problem, and Sam said the couple with the dog – us, that is – should speak first, best of all about the Azores, since everyone knew we had never been there. The rims of volcanoes rise out of the sea there, I said.

434
Incredible how differently mountains are seen. Ski slopes, investment opportunities, holiday regions, hunting grounds, places for climbing expeditions up to the sky, ursine paradise. Plus the grottoes and caves, and make sure to laugh at the innards of the various-sized monsters with your mouth closed. Do not show your teeth.

435
A clear contrast to the volcano rims in the Atlantic is the Guiana Highlands, a region that Lucius claims for himself, and he says when he hears the word plateau all that comes to mind is these ancient highlands, nothing else, as though the words plateau and the high, flattened region of Guiana were interchangeable. The mountains are a third as old as the earth, flat at the top, an unending ancient theatrical stage.

436
I do not know what it might mean that I feel drawn to Siberia, partly to the rockscape on the Lena. The Lena is the thirteenth longest river in the world; in other words, rivers flow in competition with respect to their length, just as mountains compete with regard to their height. The Lena is the thirteenth longest river in the world, and thus well ahead of the Volga, the Danube or the Rhône. This is a statistical statement, only partially linked to my north-north-east ideas. The Lena makes me think of the endlessly wide, ice-bound delta in the long winter months, of the old

languages, including in the adjacent mountainscapes, and I point to this huge region the way that Spaniard in the bodega pointed us in the direction of his dream city of Santiago de Compostela.

437
Just as sleeping primaeval creatures are stretching and awakening beneath the glaciers, the Siberian permafrost too is subsiding, and the eternal viruses and bacteria are returning to life.

438
There were overlaps in the choice of mountain themes. Milly, carefree and easily irritated at the same time, who was only once part of our mountain conversations, thought it unfair that I rather than she had first mentioned Siberia, without ever seeing the mountainscapes there, whereas she been on a five-day excursion to the region and had photos to show us. And then she showed them on her laptop. Everyone is a hoarder of photos, squirrelling away their own pictures or selected landscapes from the internet. In Milly's photos we saw her dark, even face in pale fur hats and several people beside her. Then there were mountain contours and lorries, because they were travelling by lorry, and while she scrolled through her photos it occurred to me that I had originally wanted to start a diary or at least a booklet on the subject of the east. The east is an emotive term. The west is a world in itself, the east another world. The east and the west. First I would have mentioned the Eastern and Western Alps, tourist regions, war regions. Then I would have moved further east, and north-northeast as well, and in the end I would have gathered some loaded opinions.

439
Postcard to self: A Vietnamese man falls in love with a Portuguese woman. They live together for fifty years, often arguing; they are happy, and one dies shortly after the other. Not at the same time. The surviving Portuguese woman notes that the two of them had pushed together the countries and the tectonic plates.

440
No one need go down on their knees before the gigantic Himalayan region, and nor must they rejoice, Lucius says, who once spent three days in that mountainland at a conference, and whether he was really there is not a serious question either way. We have covered that already, he says; he could get more insight on the basis of the available data and images and information than from a fleeting visit. He has weathered the weather, though, that much is for sure, and he has lasting images in his mind's eye. Commonly, he ought to speak of an uplifting impression, as if the height of the mountains and the uplifted feeling went hand in hand, which is not the case; quite the contrary. The actual heights were oppressive.

441
Rose-pink salt from Pakistan is sold as Himalayan salt. It is an officially registered trade name.

442
It would be best to flip open the globe to get an overview of the mountainscapes on a single level, Lucius said, and he began tracing mountain silhouettes in mid-air with his outstretched right hand. In the east he raised his hand high, high, high for the Himalayas, to their left the complicated

broad Altai range, then after a relatively flat stretch heading west, he indicated several bloated spots and the Caucasus to the southwest; he swung his hand on, flat, flat, slightly higher, much higher; in the west he came far beyond the Alps, and then his hand turned to the elevations further north. Incidentally, the flying hand dived deep on the west coast of Europe, to the mountain demons beneath the sea; he dived enormously deep, yet still his flipped-open earth had not reached the Andes or the Australian hills. Then he'd had enough of landscape palpating.

443
The oldest mountains are in the southeast of Africa, he said hesitatingly, suddenly subdued. I would never have thought he could lose his mood so abruptly. He was bipolar, he explained, sometimes one way, sometimes another. Shortly before he came to speak of the oldest mountains, he told me, he had thought once again that mountains too are economic territories. And then all he could do was growl, and there was no point any more to his landscape palpations.

444
There were more melancholy laments and burning remarks, not just from him.

445
I should like to know from what point of view I'd be interested in the broad, expansive landscapes of the Altai Mountains or the Caucasus if I were Japanese or an Arab or an inhabitant of the Siberian territories; which specific regions I would seek there.

446
For simplicity's sake, we shall divide up the mountain ranges between us and earmark the reddish rocks in Petra for Sam, for now. The monumental red pillars and portals carved directly into the stone look as if a person could stride deep inside a mountain, but in most cases the inviting constructions are backdrops, formerly sacred backdrops, sacred mock-ups. Gravestones, artworks for the deceased. Architecture for the storage of the dead, at the same time a symbol of victory in life, and naturally the finds in Petra are a diary, a millennia-old diary.

447
The Pyrenees are audacious, the Alps are European and hence central, often harsh and stuck-up. The Carpathians are not only rich in forest, though they are, and treacherous, including from a political point of view, as it turns out. Above all, however, they are prepared, something I cannot explain in detail, and like all mountain ranges they are constantly changing, so it is pointless to set their description in stone; there is no point carving these stone structures' characteristics in stone. Aside from a few beasts and arrogant features, there are also worldly-wise stoics among the mountain ranges, and bitter, embittered or relaxed bony ranges; and one should never annoy the Altai.

448
These character sketches apply not only to mountain ranges, not only to fated communities of identical-looking forms, but also to individual mountains. Some mountains have – to use a classical formulation – a Janus face. They have at least two faces, in profile and full frontal.

449
Manu has collected words for describing the world of mountains, and the game goes like this (if it is a game): each of us has to pick an elevation or a mountain range and imagine it or look it up on the internet, so as to choose the fitting description from the following incomplete list. And each of us can add our own epithet, as long as we've studied our object for long enough to choose the epithet fairly.

Here is the list: giant, skeleton, ghost, freak, monster, sample (demonstration model), cenotaph, block, bulwark, foreigner, hunk, chunk, scrap, heap; frank, hollow, inexorable, dissolute, timeless, ancient, mighty, portly, woozy, gnarled, crooked, wary, devious, deadly, harmless, stable, worldly, loveable, splintery, boastful, impassive, famous, lucrative, brazen; gold-digging site, restricted zone, secret zone, military site.

Depending on the structure of the mountains and mountain ranges, the list can be expanded,

450
and of course, words that represent and present a mountain place themselves, distractingly, in front of the mountain.

451
Presenting mountains as vain is a misrepresentation.

452
A group of friends are out hunting in the hunting grounds and poachers are also on the move, and while the latter

have good instincts, know the sectors they scour, know the risky clearings and the adverse rocks further up that call for firmness of foot, are all clever scouts – they must never forget that they themselves are fair game. They have skilfully evaded the hunting party. But then, all at once, the poachers run into a band of smugglers. The smugglers are also excellent at scouting, and they have spotted each other simultaneously. It is a macabre situation. What tactic to pursue? They hesitate a while,

453

and the rescue of the animals is a chapter of its own, a tragedy. This time the victims are hares and small creatures.

454

I do not have an opinion or a judgement on Mont Blanc. It does exist, the main statement is that it exists, and it too looks different from every viewing point.

455

For the Dachstein, I have an ambassador who passes me occasional information, and I'm sure he wouldn't reprimand me too harshly if I were to make a false claim about the massif. I once said that the Dachstein stood correctly but was not perfectly formed, and all he did was gulp. For years, he has spent the summer months making daily notes on a mountain pasture while taking care of goats and calves, and it has occurred to me a few times that it would be good to concentrate on a single mountain world, to stick to just one mountain; he often travels in the winter months, though.

456
To resettle or not to venture a step away from an old spot, to put down roots, to stink from the roots up. They say fish stink from the head down, so something must be up with the head if a person insists on putting down roots, no matter whether the saying about the stinking fish is true or not.

457
It has not rained since the storm; it could be cause for concern, and it is, but I shall leave the climate to Lucius, though he barely speaks about the weather these days, since he was accused (by me) of going off on scientific tangents on the subject. I can only hope he notes down the weather activities for himself,

458
but the only related term in my notes is weatherbooking. I could retrospectively conjure up some memories and describe the sky as indigo, ultramarine, azure, dark blue, glacier blue, stone grey and concrete grey, and when that African sand was in the air a yellow shade joined them. Sunset red is already well known.

Once, I was at a bus stop in Crete at around four in the morning, if I remember correctly, or at any rate it was pitch dark to start with; I was standing at the bus stop, and all at once the black sky above me was flooded with red in a matter of seconds, the black all glowing red before the sun broke through, and immediately after that it was light altogether. A seconds-long spectacle. The sunrise has its characteristics in every area, and it takes a whole lot of effort not to chase after the variants; everyone has an insatiable hunger to see the sunrise in as many places as possible, I assume, and to remember the light conditions.

459
How on earth, how can a person possibly keep several diaries simultaneously and side by side!

460
Ruth had gone to ground after our first pie convention. We looked for her in vain for a while, then Sam had the right suspicion and called up my coach, whom he got hold of in Grignan, in the Mont Ventoux area. She told him Ruth had turned up unexpectedly at her place with no luggage, and all she had said was that she was news-sick, sick from the news. She had set out in Lucerne immediately after the midday news bulletin, sick of the news, her nerves exposed. Now she wouldn't come to the telephone, only passing on the message that she was pale, pale and colourless outside and in, and the coach explained that Ruth was now getting good at not listening; she was not going to a doctor, she was going on walks.

461
What was when exactly. We can skip this question.

462
Postcard to the coach: It would make sense to start separate notes on animals, on dogs with bears' eyes, on alpacas, onagers, on different species of cloven-hoofed animals and on grey and red squirrels.

463
Increasingly, we all sit for days at our monitors, staring at our screens, getting sick, going to the doctor – and then falling in love. One man's eyes are burning, his doctor comes close to examine him, the patient sees her hands, feels the heat of those hands; she leans forward and that's when it almost gets personal. An orthopaedist leans over his patient, she has back pain, he and she are alone in the midst of the digital era, he breathes and she has not been questioned as intensely for years, in such togetherness. The patients sit down, lie down, and talk about their bodies. All the things they could say! Pent-up statements. Ringing in their ears, lost lovers, fears in the afternoon or at night, and the doctors ask more questions, look the patients in the eye. It is very nearly intimate.

464
Everyone has long since known it, but said nothing. Everyone knew it.

465
The losers slowly descend the slope. The mountain's ridgeline can be made out high above their heads, and the losers, more than a hundred people, come ever lower, never showing a frown. A murmuring, slow troop of losers.

466
Manu was retouching photos in her clink, biting her lips. She had this rush job from a detective agency, she said, which I was probably not supposed to believe. In any case, while she worked I sat in her back room with Sam and Lucius and watched a report on the Altai Mountains.

Expansive landscapes, scraped-off mountains in the distance, a gravelly sand-coloured region. Barely any green but still plenty of sheep, wonderful horses and eagles.

The film was about training eagles. Many serious people in brightly coloured clothing gathered for a sporting competition, men with eagles. The eagles, which had to perform a precisely stipulated flight manoeuvre, could have flown away from the tournament but a long-standing dialogue existed between them and their keepers; they belonged together.

467
The main thing is that the stories and notes are not too well rounded.

468
I still like it best to see all notes as playing cards, to shuffle them, deal a few of the cards to six or seven players and leave the rest in the stack on the table. The players have a random selection of text in their hand, just for example: notes on colours, languages, mountain images and roast lamb, and now the idea is to link together as many texts as possible in a halfway plausible way, latch them all on to each other. The latched-together cards are laid face-up on the table, and after that the player can take more face-down notes from the stack.

469
After not long at all, two policemen come along and talk about illegal gambling, show their search warrant, find nothing suspicious but still confiscate the cards.

470
In the same way that magnetic splinters (iron filings) align themselves to the attracting force, all the notes must fit together at the end. If they don't fit, I'm out of luck. (But why should they not fit, what does not fit mean?)

471
The iron filings are on the table, attracting each other magnetically and producing a picture. What they are saying with the picture, heaven knows. (No one knows, not one person knows.)

472
I remember a travelling philosopher whom I shall not mention by name, so as not to offend this upstanding if deceased wise man. He was briefly in China, and afterwards he described the Chinese understanding of marriage, namely that couples there do not want to fulfil themselves as couples but as individuals, each for themselves. That is a formidable statement, and I wonder whether Chinese couples might be rather cool or disinterested in their partners, or are they self-centred or deeply tolerant? This travel note at least leads to such considerations, which I shall book as a bonus, but how could that traveller fathom married couples' attitudes in such a short time, or verify them, as we say these days? Had interpreters relayed conversations? Was he quoting passages from a text translated for him?

473
Travel journals are out of the question. There is no point in multiple separate entries each with their own subject,

simply because the topics get easily entangled even if I try to isolate them, and in the end Sam's idea with the walkable rooms, as he drew it, is a clear solution, no matter how the contents, previously called topics, are put in each room. The good thing about this idea is that the contents are put on show and are walkable.

474
The crude, the smooth and the stony or wooded mountain ranges correspond with one another and drift closer together. They're moving ever closer together. Some of them get stranded, though, unsuccessful and inconsequential, they do not touch, no one can transport them and nor can they move out of the way, and while the others keep moving closer together, these ones are ploughed under.

475
Mount Narodnaya is the highest elevation in the Urals. The mountain looks frightful, like bent old bones. It was discovered as the highest elevation in this not random mountain range only in 1927. What is discovered, here! Who discovered what so late? (What was when?) The region is home to Samoyed, Mansi and Khanty people with related, almost shared languages, who have been living in the Urals for much more than a hundred years; the people settled there for millennia were once undiscovered along with their mountains, as were their languages. Hardly anyone used to care about languages anyway.

476
There were circular villages in the Urals, millennia ago. In these cleverly arranged settlements, gold was mined from

the rock. What kinds of peoples with what kinds of pasts dug for gold?

477
At the excavation sites, they made weighty discoveries. I remember a film about these villages on the eastern edge of the Urals, or rather in the mountains, but I can find no trace of it on the internet, which means my own memory of the primordial gold rush, the gold ideas and the architecturally interesting places is a bonus.

478
Concerning today's gold excavations, however, I did find a revealing instruction (on the internet): 'Before entering these discovery sites, permission should be obtained from the operator or owner.'

479
When did the word gold first appear in what languages? Criminalistics says that gold, which in German is connected to gelb, i.e. yellow, migrated from a Semitic language to the southern Urals. In the northern part of the slim mountain range, they took longer to pick up a suitable word.

480
In the Subpolar Urals and the Polar Urals, they didn't dig for metals or gems. They didn't break the rock. In the entire mountain range the locals were fishermen, huntsmen and bird-catchers (the grammatically fitting term would be birdsmen), but in the south they were gold-diggers too.

481
If I am correctly oriented, the Urals are brimming with fish languages. The fish is a reference point, found similarly in all language variants. Fish ate their way into the thinnest of cracks in the rock.

482
For Russians, the highest mountain in the Urals is a she. Every mountain is female in Russian; perhaps a pointed breast inspired the idea. For Uralic speakers, however, a mountain is a mountain and that's that. They have never included questions of he, she or it in their considerations. Mountains, rivers, fishes have no genders, and this deliberation (non-deliberation) holds a world in itself.

483
I have spent restless nights in conjunction with languages, not only due to Uralic and thus also Finno-Ugric, which have relatives all the way to Siberia, and not only due to Basque, whose past is neglected. I could list further neglects. From a statistical perspective, these restless nights make up a considerable percentage of my life.

484
Recently, Lucius has tried to calculate how many flight hours each individual worldwide is entitled to make, should air traffic be at least slightly curbed but everyone be allowed to fly once. I must have used up my own hours long ago.

485
Years ago, I sat for a while in the cockpit on a flight from Seoul to Zürich, directly behind the pilot and co-pilot,

and looked down at first on the Asian side, in good light conditions, on what seemed to me a flat landscape; then we flew towards rocky territory and crossed it. We crossed the Ural mountain fold, which does not really divide the continents and looks lower from above than it really is.

486
The co-pilot told me the altitude we were flying at and explained we had crossed the Urals between Nizhny Tagil and Perm. Then at home I found out the Mansi word tagil means rich in water, and Mansi is an almost extinct, half-sleeping language.

487
Postcard to self: The city of Nizhny Tagil is located on the River Tagil on the eastern side of the lower third of the Urals, with a view (distant view) of Asia. Some inhabitants still speak Mansi today. Mansi, in turn, is one of the Uralic languages that have relatives up to the Polar Urals.

488
Manu says all words are pictures. We nod, and I say she should photograph words too.

489
The Urals are a slim extended strip of mountains full of rivers and waterways, a strip that leaves a deep impression on the observer and aims to awaken emotions. The Uralic languages have always had a similar intention: they are out for the sound.

490
Sam and Manu speak Basque. They both spent a year in the Pyrenees, and they both know how it is to leave the Central European languages and dive into another world of ideas. It renders quirks, tricks, talents and statements of familiar languages visible too.

491
Languages too have a nucleus and thus a fundamental orientation, and although languages change, are constantly changing, it is possible to poke around in the old language forms, to search, to reach an original mood,

492
and that word mood: I could replace it with interest, with fundamental interest.

493
Sam shall ride on horseback across the entire mountain range, and with a tambourine in his hand he will proclaim, or rather sing (for a better sound), that there are and there were highly gifted languages in the Urals, some of which have been urged into half-sleep and now keep their mouths shut.

494
These language variants help with spatial orientation, proclaims Sam, and rides on.

495
I recently read that our neural nerve centres are responsible for orientation, including in our social surroundings, and

thus for emotions in our spatial surroundings, and thus for our languages.

496
Postcard: It is not irrelevant which languages were and are spoken in the Urals, otherwise the language variants in the Alps, for instance, would not matter.

497
In the Alps, too, lie old chunks of language, legacies that are treated more leniently in part, but only in part. A majority of the old possibilities have been ploughed under.

498
Postcard: The matter of the Ural languages is a Western in the east. The main thing is that they exist.

499
A few years ago, a meteorite crashed to the ground close to Yekaterinburg in the southeastern Urals and injured more than a thousand, and even those not injured were marked for years, ravaged by the meteorite. Violence is violence. The locals lost their windows in freezing wintry temperatures, the glass shattered by the pressure of the meteorite's crash. The event happened at a great distance. The newsreaders' reports were relaxed and mentioned that a meteorite of the same size might also hit other places, though similar disasters only occur every thousand years.

500
Foxes, meerkats, birches were all crushed to death.

501
After this news I was travelling in the Urals; near Sverdlovsk I met Vladimir Mayakovsky, who generally called himself I. He said, or he wrote, that he was every I, all I that existed was he. Fantastic. We stood facing each other. I said to him: I too. He stared at me, first, then turned his back on me mutely. Perhaps it was my Russian. I only know ten to twenty wonderful words, and sadly I do not pronounce them quite right.

To make him listen to me, I asked him loudly why he was travelling in the Urals, of all places. He turned back to me, for both he and I were only in the mountains in our minds. We poked at the ground, seeking the traces of former inhabitants, seeking people (and finding several Is).

502
A few stories of these Is we uncovered, we wanted to latch on to other I-stories and construct relationships between them; we, the keepers of the Urals.

503
The relatively bare Urals are a long line in the atlas, running from top to bottom, north to south. The left-hand side is European, the right-hand side is Asian. That says a great deal. The mountain range is stuffed with ores and gold deposits, not to be sniffed at, but as far east as the Urals may be, people still like to push them further east, deport them.

504
The Mansi and other Uralic speakers were eternally patronised and treated as oafish clowns, especially until

around two hundred years ago and before, when everyone considered only their own language right and accountable, whereby some, individually and groupwise, still swear by only their own language today.

505
At times, these so-called clowns had had enough of it, had taken too many blows and had to keep their mouths shut way too often. But they had an answer at the ready. Courage acts against a fall, close your mouth and go for it, they hummed and they grumbled and growled, except they barely protested, at most by taking flight to their songs, to their mourning elegies, which could suddenly flip into joy and still do. The songs echo non-stop in the long thin mountain range. To claim that the newly arrived Russian tones overlaying and supplanting the Uralic were not melodic would be witless, but it is a shame about the Uralic songs.

506
We're investigating in all directions. It's purely routine.

507
The uniformed men inch quietly closer, with bent knees and brandished guns. They have been called out to rescue two central Uralic languages. They are dead or half-dead and must be protected from assailants: that is the men's mission. But the two are alive, invulnerable, immune, merely lacking a certain intensity, and sometimes they're joyless and tired; above all they lack trust, so they hide from the uniformed men and in the end no one and nothing is saved.

508
In between, I had intended to ask or request Woody Allen to make a sequel to his Paris and Rome movies, set in the Urals. I imagine he would mix the necessary gravity with flippancy and even include short passages of Russian dialogue, even though Russian is supplanting the older languages.

509
Are languages utensils?

510
Postcard to self: For Central Europeans, the Urals are located far in the east, and pushing the range further east has long been a key objective.

511
This mountain range belongs to me. I stake my claim.

512
Postcard to Ruth: If the Urals are supposed to be the border to Europe, then Europe (a Greek woman, as we know) is a lady without an abdomen. We must draw the lady's contours.

513
Mountain-shoving, stone-shoving, the mountain ranges inching closer together by push and by shove, and along the way the minerals inside them slip and slide out of place, the gold, the ores, the sleeping gems, various salts and rare earths.

514
Once again, we spent a day bent over different atlases.

layout plan appearance escapade fathom zenith ruse guest performance southern slope frantic erosion firn peak alluvial fan bridlebit abyssal rock chasm herdsman exile gradient milestone karst bearing catacomb sidelong glance ignominy spectrum tectonic number magic constraints bandit agent conflict circumstantial evidence sparking up forking out pilgriming clogging up limiting primaeval state stronghold unplanned prong tapping raised hide profane patronage tiering veteran trendsetter edict serious flanking feigning getting even starving failing donating blasphemer scheme interim unquenchable isolated rubble approval freeloader offence plotter calamity dissonance patriot hermitage decorative supervision restricted zone obtrusive gold scale simmering fallow buck flash light emergency trait delusion clumsy subdomain spoor meadow sideswipe slow motion

515

I wanted to pour myself a whisky when Lucius handed
me a note, a few lines about the Scottish Highlands.
In geological terms they are older than the Atlantic, it said.
A rather strange comparison, as Lucius thought too.
He got the details from the internet.

The hunched highlands, a good whisky region, old
landscape of water of life! Vodka too means little water.

( ) ( ) p prototype

poetry / prose / interdisciplinary projects / anthologies

Creating new possibilities in the publishing of fiction and poetry through a flexible, interdisciplinary approach and the production of unique and beautiful books.

Prototype is an independent publisher working across genres and disciplines, committed to discovering and sharing work that exists outside the mainstream.

Each publication is unique in its form and presentation, and the aesthetic of each object is considered critical to its production.

Prototype strives to increase audiences for experimental writing, as the home for writers and artists whose work requires a creative vision not offered by mainstream literary publishers.

In its current, evolving form, Prototype consists of 4 strands of publications:

(type 1 – poetry)
(type 2 – prose)
(type 3 – interdisciplinary projects)
(type 4 – anthologies) including an annual anthology of new work, *PROTOTYPE*.

Forthcoming

(type 2 – prose)

Book of Mutter by Kate Zambreno (2025)
Appendix Project by Kate Zambreno (2025)
Fair by Jen Calleja (2025)
Happiness by Yuri Felsen, trans. Bryan Karetnyk (2025)
Mr Outside by Caleb Klaces (2025)

Back Catalogue

(type 1 – poetry)

Plainspeak by Astrid Alben (2019)
Safe Metamorphosis by Otis Mensah (2020)
Republic Of Dogs/Republic Of Birds by Stephen Watts (2016/2020)
Home by Emily Critchley (2021)
Away From Me by Caleb Klaces (2021)
Path Through Wood by Sam Buchan-Watts (2021)
Two Twin Pipes Sprout Water by Lila Matsumoto (2021)
Deltas by Leonie Rushforth (2022)
Island mountain glacier by Anne Vegter, trans. Astrid Alben (2022)
Little Dead Rabbit by Astrid Alben (2022)
Emblem by Lucy Mercer (2022)
Twenty-Four Hours by Stephen Watts (2022)
A History by Dan Burt (2022)
Journeys Across Breath: Poems 1975–2005 by Stephen Watts (2022)
Artifice by Lavinia Singer (2023)
Incubation: a space for monsters by Bhanu Kapil (2023)
Monochords by Yannis Ritsos, trans. Paul Merchant, with Chiara Ambrosio (2023)
Virgula by Sasja Janssen, trans. Michele Hutchison (2024)
The Grimoire of Grimalkin by Sascha Aurora Akhtar (2024)
rock flight by Hasib Hourani (2024)

(type 2 – prose)

Fatherhood by Caleb Klaces (2019)
I'm Afraid That's All We've Got Time For by Jen Calleja (2020)
The Boiled in Between by Helen Marten (2020)

Along the River Run by Paul Buck (2020)
Lorem Ipsum by Oli Hazzard (2021)
The Weak Spot by Lucie Elven (2021)
Deceit by Yuri Felsen, trans. Bryan Karetnyk (2022)
Our Last Year by Alan Rossi (2022)
Vehicle: a verse novel by Jen Calleja (2023)
Lori & Joe by Amy Arnold (2023)
Pleasure Beach by Helen Palmer (2023)
The Earth is Falling by Carmen Pellegrino, trans. Shaun Whiteside (2024)
Prairie, Dresses, Art, Other by Danielle Dutton (2024)
The Seers by Sulaiman Addonia (2024)

(type 3 – interdisciplinary projects)
alphabet poem: for kids! by Emily Critchley, Michael Kindellan & Alison Honey Woods (2020)
The sea is spread and cleaved and furled by Ahren Warner (2020)
Songs for Ireland by Robert Herbert McClean (2020)
microbursts by Elizabeth Reeder & Amanda Thomson (2021)
Sorcerer by Ed Atkins & Steven Zultanski (2023)
i will pay to make it bigger by Ahren Warner (2024)

(type 4 – anthologies)
Try To Be Better ed. Sam Buchan-Watts & Lavinia Singer (2019)
PROTOTYPE 1 (2019)
PROTOTYPE 2 (2020)
Intertitles: An anthology at the intersection of writing & visual art, ed. Jess Chandler, Aimee Selby, Hana Noorali & Lynton Talbot (2021)
PROTOTYPE 3 (2021)
PROTOTYPE 4 (2022)
Strangers Within: Documentary as Encounter, ed. Therese Hennigsen & Juliette Joffé (2022)
PROTOTYPE 5 (2023)
Seven Rooms, ed. Dominic J. Jaeckle & Jess Chandler (2023)
PROTOTYPE 6 (2023)

Some writers aspire to build castles in the air, but Zsuzsanna Gahse dares to deconstruct far more fundamental geological edifices. In Mountainish *she approaches – through a series of impressionistic fragments – a distinctly individual understanding of altitude and terrain. Clichés crumble to reveal startling new vistas. A generous and perceptive gathering of kaleidoscopic observations on landscape and the languages that echo through them. Katy Derbyshire's translation is clear as air at 15,000 feet.*

Nancy Campbell

In Mountainish, *Gahse directs her reader through 515 notes, making it clear with great elegance and wit that an escape to the mountains is not an escape from the self; that the unconscious is bound to landscape and reverberations; that words haunt like ghosts; that the echo of self cannot be avoided. Each note is a story and each mountain or what is like a mountain is a language; it is a matter of orientation. I have marked the pages of this brilliant book as though it were an atlas. It is a place to which I am compelled to return, even if I might be smashed apart.*

Sharon Kivland

Zsuzsanna Gahse reflects on questions of perception, language, art and the digital world. Mountains are dissected and even playfully moved like chess pieces. Words also wander, change their sound, are smoothed, plastered and hollowed out. Gahse criticises the illusion of a 'pristine', clean homeland and opens up the view.

Jens-Peter Kusch, *Viceversa Literatur*

Gahse collects portraits of people and regions, is interested in colours and colour changes, things and their names, languages, language changes and the disappearance of languages, the economic conditions in mountain regions, tourism and much more. The presentation is a kaleidoscope of mountain landscapes and disparate things.

Oswald Burger, *Südkurier*

Mountainish *is an idiosyncratic book – an unusual combination of intellectual speculation, delicate observation, and sustained flippancy. In Zsuzsanna Gahse's Alps you might find a group of buses doing a dance routine or a new theory of language; friends discussing cave art or an unfortunate donkey plunging to her death.*

Daisy Hildyard

Somewhere in the Swiss Alps – amidst rock, scree, lakes and caves, between ochre and red, and in the place where vowels fly through the mountain skies – lies Mountainish. *Zsuzsanna Gahse's observations, at once sharp and supple, challenge us to look, to listen – to look and listen all over again. I loved it!*

Amy Arnold

Mountainish by Zsuzsanna Gahse
Published by Prototype in 2025

First published as *Bergisch teils farblos* in Austria by Edition Korrespondenzen in 2021.

 A CIP record for this book is available from the British Library.

Design by Matthew Stuart & Andrew Walsh-Lister (Traven T. Croves)
Typeset in Marist by Seb McLauchlan
Printed in the UK by TJ Books

Published with the support of the Swiss Arts Council Pro Helvetia and the Canton of Thurgau lottery fund.

ISBN 978-1-913513-64-1

(type 2 – prose)
www.prototypepublishing.co.uk
@prototypepubs

prototype publishing
71 oriel road
london e9 5sg
uk

swiss arts council
prohelvetia

Thurgau
Lotteriefonds